Skye Munros
The walker's guide to bagging the Cuillin summits

by Adrian Trendall

JUNIPER HOUSE, MURLEY MOSS,
OXENHOLME ROAD, KENDAL, CUMBRIA LA9 7RL
www.cicerone.co.uk

© Adrian Trendall 2026
First edition 2026
ISBN: 978 1 78631 204 4
eISBN: 978 1 78765 236 1

Cicerone's EU representative for GPSR compliance is Easy Access System Europe, Mustamäe tee 50, 10621 Tallinn, Estonia. Email gpsr.requests@easproject.com.

Printed in China on responsibly sourced paper on behalf of Latitude Press Ltd.
A catalogue record for this book is available from the British Library.
All photographs are by the author unless otherwise stated.

Maps are reproduced with permission from HARVEY Maps, www.harveymaps.co.uk

Updates to this guide

While every effort is made by our authors to ensure the accuracy of guidebooks as they go to print, changes can occur during the lifetime of an edition. Any updates that we know of for this guide will be on the Cicerone website (www.cicerone.co.uk/1204/updates), so please check before planning your trip. We also advise that you check information about such things as transport, accommodation and shops locally. Even rights of way can be altered over time. We are always grateful for information about any discrepancies between a guidebook and the facts on the ground, sent by email to updates@cicerone.co.uk.

Register your book: To sign up to receive free updates, special offers and GPX files where available, create a Cicerone account and register your purchase via the 'My Account' tab at www.cicerone.co.uk.

Front cover: Sgurr Thormaid catching early morning sunlight with the twin summits of Sgurr a Ghreadaidh in the background (Routes 2 and 3)

Contents

INTRODUCTION 6
The Cuillin Munros 7
The challenge 9
Order of difficulty 10
Stacking the odds in your favour 11
Inspiration 16
Preparation and training 17
Kit list 19
Logistics 22
Geology 22
Environmental considerations 23
Grades 24
Using this guide 25

THE MUNROS 27
Sgurr nan Eag, 924m 28
Sgurr Dubh Mor, 944m 28
Sgurr Alasdair, 993m 30
Sgurr Mhic Choinnich, 948m 33
Sgurr Dearg: The Inaccessible Pinnacle, 986m 34
Sgurr na Banachdich, 965m 36
Sgurr a' Ghreadaidh, 973m 39
Sgurr a' Mhadaidh, 918m 41
Bruach na Frithe, 958m 42
Am Basteir, 935m 43
Sgurr nan Gillean, 965m 46
Bla Bheinn, 928m 48

Abseil of the tricky section of the West Ridge Sgurr nan Gillean. Narrow bit of ridge is to the right of the figure (Route 1)

Warning! Climbing and scrambling can be dangerous

Climbing and scrambling can be dangerous activities carrying a risk of personal injury or death. It should be undertaken only by those with a full understanding of the risks and with the training and experience to evaluate them. Mountaineers should be appropriately equipped for the routes undertaken. Whilst every care and effort has been taken in the preparation of this book, the user should be aware that conditions are highly variable and can change quickly. Holds may become loose or fall off, rockfall can affect the character of the route, and in winter, snow and avalanche conditions must be carefully considered. These can materially affect the seriousness of a scramble, tour or expedition.

Therefore, except for any liability which cannot be excluded by law, neither Cicerone nor the author accept liability for damage of any nature including damage to property, personal injury or death arising directly or indirectly from the information in this book.

High on the south-west flank of Sgurr Alasdair with Sgurr Sgumain in the background (Route 4)

Skye Munros

Introduction

Sir Hugh Munro's list of 'Tables Giving All The Scottish Mountains Exceeding 3000 Feet in Height' was published in 1891. The Munros represent a big challenge with peaks spread far and wide across Scotland, but perhaps the biggest challenge is the Cuillin Munros on the Isle of Skye. This book provides the information needed to tackle the Cuillin Munros.

Skye is a popular tourist destination but Munroists will arrive with their sights firmly set on twelve summits. The Black Cuillin is Scotland's premier mountain range: Alpine-like peaks without the altitude. Jagged peaks are linked by airy ridges and separated by huge coires. It is a beautiful range and a tough challenge, involving not just rough walking but also scrambling, climbing and even an abseil or two.

The aim of this book is to provide a one-stop knowledge base for the Cuillin Munros. At one extreme, it's aimed at the 'scaredy cats' who are dreading having to do the Cuillin Munros to 'compleat'. At the other end of the scale, it provides enough information for the more experienced to tackle at least some or perhaps all of the Munros under their own steam. This book will help Munroists to arrive on Skye as well prepared as possible, with the odds stacked in their favour.

Sunrise from Sgurr na Banachdich, with Sgurr Thormaid catching the sunlight and the twin summits of Sgurr a' Ghreadaidh beyond (Routes 2 and 3)

The Cuillin Munros are a big challenge but a rewarding one. Expect to work hard, perhaps expect to be scared, but picture the rewards once all twelve are in the bag and you are celebrating with a drink in Seumas' Bar at Sligachan.

The Cuillin Munros

Munros are defined as Scottish mountains over 3000ft or 914.4m in height on the Scottish Mountaineering Club (SMC) list of Munros. The SMC also lists Munro Tops, which are also Scottish peaks over 3000ft but with insufficient separation to be identified as Munros. Currently the list contains 282 Munros and 226 Munro Tops.

There are twelve Munros (and nine Munro Tops) on Skye, and the nature of them reflects the geography and geology of the Cuillin mountains. Eleven are located on (or just off) the main Cuillin Ridge, with Bla Bheinn being an outlier high above Loch Slapin. Some of the easier Cuillin Munros are just tough walks but the majority are a far cry from their mainland counterparts, involving scrambling, graded rock climbs and abseils.

For many Munroists, the Cuillin will present a formidable challenge. Skye and its Munros offers a big obstacle to those wanting to do all the Munros, which is why many people leave them to last and/or choose to hire a guide.

A variety of factors set the Cuillin Munros apart from their mainland brethren:

1. Reputation
The Cuillin Munros have a huge reputation which can be a deterrent. People can be put off by what they have heard and videos they have seen on social media, or by route descriptions and grades.

2. Exposure
Steep, rocky ground, exposed ridges and big drops combine to present a challenge totally different to that of the majority of the mainland Munros.

3. Technical terrain
While some of the easier Cuillin Munros are little more than tough walks, the rest involve much more technical terrain with a high degree of exposure. Scrambling and rock climbing skills are necessary, as well as the ability to abseil. Even on some of the easier scrambles, the terrain will often be very consequential where a slip or trip could be serious.

4. Route finding
While there may be good paths lower down, higher up most of the routes will be across scree or rocks with tracks only ill-defined at best. Lots of the mileage will be over pathless terrain where a degree of mountaineering nous and experience will be an asset.

In conditions of perfect visibility route finding may seem straightforward, but in sub-optimal conditions it will be much tougher. With so many steep drops around, spot-on navigation is essential. Precision is required,

Heading out to Sgurr Dubh Mor from Sgurr Dubh an Da Bheinn (Route 4)

so mountaineering experience must be combined with good navigational skills. The Cuillin Munros are no place to be blindly following GPX files on your phone.

All the summits are 'proper' Munros, and every ascent starts from pretty much sea level. The Cuillin Munros involve lots of height gain and loss, lots of scrambling and climbing, and lots of exposure.

The challenge

Compared to many mainland Munros, Cuillin days out may seem short in distance and time but be prepared for a lot of ascent and descent, lots of scree, and lots of easy scrambling. Then factor in more serious scrambling, as well as some climbing and abseiling.

Below are a few statistics from a typical four-day Munro course to give an idea of what is involved.

Munros	Distance	Ascent	Time
Sgurr nan Gillean Am Basteir Bruach na Frithe	14.0km	1350m	7–9hr
Sgurr a' Mhadaidh Sgurr a' Ghreadaidh	9.0km	1000m	6–7hr
Sgurr na Banachdich Inaccessible Pinnacle Sgurr Mhic Choinnich	12.0km	1400m	8–9hr
Sgurr nan Eag Sgurr Dubh Mor Sgurr Alasdair	12.5km	1450m	9–11hr

The above figures give an idea of the statistics involved but do not be put off by these figures since the Munros can be broken down into more manageable chunks.

Guides typically offer four-day courses covering all eleven Cuillin Ridge Munros. Such short courses are cost effective but demand a high degree of fitness and determination and allow little leeway for bad weather.

Order of difficulty

This is a very subjective matter and can be very personal. What one person finds easy may be terrifying for others, and the experience will depend on conditions and weather. For example, Sgurr Mhic Choinnich may seem straightforward for some people in the dry. However, in the wet the upper basalt slabs become treacherously slippery.

Start off with easier summits and see how you get on. However, do not underestimate even the easier three Cuillin Munros, because even on those navigation can be confusing in poor visibility.

1	Bruach na Frithe	Walk
2	Sgurr na Banachdich	Walk
3	Bla Bheinn	Walk
4	Sgurr nan Eag	Grade 1 scramble
5	Sgurr Alasdair	Grade 2 scramble
6	Sgurr a' Mhadaidh	Grade 2/3 scramble
7	Sgurr a' Ghreadaidh	Grade 3 scramble
8	Sgurr Dubh Mor	Grade 2 scramble
9	Am Basteir	Difficult rock climb (but Bad Step can be bypassed)
10	Sgurr nan Gillean	Grade 3 scramble
11	Sgurr Mhic Choinnich	Grade 2 scramble
12	Inaccessible Pinnacle	Moderate rock climb and an abseil

Note that the grades above are usually for the easiest routes for that Munro. However, when combining Munros, harder alternatives have to be taken. For example, the easiest route up Sgurr nan Gillean, the south-east ridge, is a grade 3 scramble. But if this peak is done in conjunction with Am Basteir it will mean ascending and descending the west ridge which is a Moderate rock climb with an abseil descent.

Sgurr Dubh Mor is ranked harder than Sgurr a' Ghreadaidh and Sgurr a' Mhadaidh because the difficulties on the latter two are primarily confined to the exit and return to/from An Dorus. The difficulties are a couple of short moves and easily protected by a rope. Conversely, Sgurr Dubh Mor is a far more remote challenge and finding the correct line can be difficult in poor visibility.

Sgurr Mhic Choinnich has been ranked higher than others despite having a lower grade because it is more exposed and more sustained, with the difficulties far longer and more continuous. Am Basteir has some awkward down climbing over the Bad Step but

Stacking the odds in your favour

View from Sgurr a' Mhadaidh (Route 2) to Loch Coruisk with Bla Bheinn (Route 5) top left

this is literally only a couple of metres and is easily protected, or it can be bypassed.

Stacking the odds in your favour

Weather and conditions

For many people, especially those booking holidays and guides in advance, weather and conditions are very much down to the luck of the draw. Fine weather in itself has an added feel-good factor that is impossible to quantify. It also means dry, non-slippery rock, more straightforward navigation and not being buffeted by strong winds.

If at all possible then try to come to Skye for an extended period of time so you can pick and choose days according to the forecasts.

The period between May and late September gives the most likely chance of favourable conditions. May and late September have the added bonus of having less chance of midges, whereas June has the longest daylight hours. Avoiding the school holidays is recommended if possible.

Any earlier than May, there could well be serious amounts of snow remaining high up. Autumn often has settled periods of stable weather but the days are noticeably shorter.

Skye's maritime climate can make or break your trip. Given clear and dry conditions, you may wonder what the fuss is about. The rock will be dry and grippy, and good visibility will facilitate easy navigation. But should you get poor conditions then the challenge will be a quantum leap harder.

Skye Munros

Genghis and Mac in inclement weather at the trig point on Bruach na Frithe (Route 1)

In the wet, the rock, especially basalt, will be slippery, navigation will be a real challenge, and progress will be slow and unpleasant. Conversely, too good weather can also be difficult. In hot conditions you will need to carry extra water, and with little shade on the ridge it will be a battle to escape from the relentless sun. Sunburn and dehydration can become problems.

Ideal conditions would be dry weather with the tops cloud-free, giving good views but more importantly easier for navigation. Higher clouds to filter the sun and keep things cooler would be ideal, as would a breeze to keep any midges at bay. High pressure and high clouds would be perfect.

Preferred forecast is the Met Office's Mountain Forecast for the North West Highlands, which can be accessed from www.metoffice.gov.uk. You can select individual Munros and get a forecast for the coming week. Things to take particular note of include the amount of precipitation, the temperatures, and wind direction and speed.

It is always worth checking as many forecasts as possible. Other popular forecasts include the Mountain Weather Information Service (www.mwis.org.uk), Windy.com (www.windy.com) and Yr (www.yr.no/en).

Navigation

Should you be lucky and experience wall-to-wall sunshine then you may wonder why people make such a fuss about navigation. If visibility is poor then navigation can be a challenge.

Stacking the odds in your favour

Summit of Sgurr a' Mhadaidh in good visibility (above) and in poor visibility (below) (Route 2)

The terrain is extremely complex and you may well come across evidence of people who have been lost. Signs of wear and tear, tracks leading nowhere and abandoned slings for abseiling from all tell of previous epics. In theory, narrow ridges sound hard to get lost on, but in reality it is hard to envision a more complex navigational scenario.

View to the Cuillin Ridge from Bla Bheinn (Route 5)

Spot-on navigation is crucial since there are steep drops all around and an error of a few metres could have serious consequences. By far the best map to use is the Harvey Superwalker XT25 Skye: The Cuillin. It is incredibly detailed with a huge amount of information but even maps at this scale (1:12,500) cannot show every minor detail so use it with care. Note that the contour intervals are at 15m with 75m index contours.

The Cuillin is notorious for magnetic rocks meaning compasses cannot always be relied upon. GPS units and phones are useful and another tool in your navigational armoury but don't be too reliant on something that could go wrong or run out of power. GPS can come into its own in poor visibility and can often help make sense of the complex topography.

If you are not overly confident as a navigator then go with a competent friend or hire a guide.

Friends and partners

Who you choose to go with is hugely important. If possible then go with somebody with personal experience of the Cuillin – somebody who knows the routes, can help put you at ease and is able to offer the security of a rope when needed.

Husbands, wives and partners are not always the best choice, especially for the more nervous or if there is a big disparity in skill levels and mental attitudes.

Guides

Consider using a local guide with experience of the area who will maximise your chances of success. Guides are not for everyone and many Munroists manage on their own, but for the more nervous, hiring a guide makes a lot of sense.

Start easy

Nothing puts people off more than failure and fear. Choose an appropriate

Stacking the odds in your favour

Munro to start with, then build your confidence and progress in small increments towards those tougher peaks. A little success can be a real confidence booster so start easy and build up.

Bite-sized chunks
Break the Cuillin Munros into days which you can easily complete. Long, tiring days are not going to boost your confidence.

The enjoyment factor
Remember, this is meant to be fun, not a battleground. Take frequent breaks, chill out, and stay hydrated and energised. Stop to take photos and admire the views.

Abseiling off the Inaccessible Pinnacle with the island of Rum in the distance (Route 3)

Local knowledge
Research as much as possible. Join the Facebook group 'All Things Cuillin', or numerous other Munro groups. Learn as much as possible about the challenge ahead. Little things, such as knowing places where you can dump poles and packs to lighten the load, can make a big difference.

Head games
The Inaccessible Pinnacle summarises the importance of head game for these Munros. If you have saved these to the end of your Muno challenge then you will almost certainly have experienced longer days, tougher days, but Skye's Munros deserve their reputation for exposure and complexity. Respect that reputation and build yourself up to it but do not be put off.

Recognise your fears, face them, and try to overcome them or at least to channel them. There is nothing irrational about being scared of heights; it is a natural survival instinct.

Repeated exposure to steep ground, starting with minimal exposure and gradually building up, will help to overcome or at least to control these fears. The fear will still be there but you will have learned to control it, to rationalise things as you learn to scramble and climb and begin to trust in the safety net provided by climbing gear. It is a joint mental and physical approach. As you get more used to exposure and become more adept at scrambling then the fear should become a bit more manageable.

Skye Munros

Each little step forwards, or upwards, will increase your confidence as you realise that you have achieved what previously would have seemed impossible. Fear management is a skill, and like any skill it can be learned. As your proficiency improves, your movement will become a bit more instinctive. Practice pays off and you will become able to move instinctively without having to really think about what you are doing.

Set goals

Once you have recognised your fears and decided to do something positive about them, then set yourself goals to work towards. Make the goals achievable so as to get early boosts to your confidence. Perhaps a simple climb or abseil at your local climbing wall would be a good start, or an easy scramble. Take easy, achievable steps so that after each mini challenge you go home feeling positive with a smile on your face.

Set your goals so you are on a path leading you to the easiest Cuillin Munros and then onwards from there. Come away from every goal with a list of positives. Things might not have been 100% perfect but take comfort from the positives. Perhaps you did not reach the top of the climb but take pride from the fact that you gave it a go.

Inspiration

Take comfort from the fact that people who have been terrified of the challenge have managed to bag the Cuillin Munros.

Donna had built up the In Pinn into an almost impossible challenge, massive doubts offsetting her very obvious ability and determination. In reality, Donna versus the In Pinn was no challenge at all. Donna faced down her nemesis and even smiled in the face of adversity.

Donna was a self-professed scaredy cat but she succeeded due to a variety of factors:

1. The main plus point was her mental stamina. Her determination to succeed countered her doubts and fears.
2. Having a trusted friend with her was a huge confidence boost, giving Donna mental and physical support. Neil was able to verbally encourage Donna and to point out crucial holds. Most important was him just being there, a presence as a confident figure nearby and ready to offer assistance.
3. Timing was crucial. The In Pinn is one of the few choke points in the Cuillin and queuing for a route then doing it in front of strangers is not a positive experience. We left 2hr earlier than any of the other guided parties so as to get it to ourselves, no queues, no pressure. The plan worked, and we were heading down for tea and cakes as other teams headed up.

Donna later sent me an email which should make encouraging reading for other scaredy cats:

'Just a message to say how grateful I am for yesterday. I really enjoyed it

Preparation and training

'Scaredy cat' Donna approaches the summit of the Inaccessible Pinnacle (Route 3)

and for someone who isn't really fit, fast or strong this is a massive achievement for me. I'm always so thankful for every hill experience but Sgurr Dearg and the In Pinn was possibly a game changer, a life-changing moment. A real lesson for me to reflect on when I think I cannot do something or achieve this or that ... well, actually, perhaps I can.

'Self-doubt, fear and lack of confidence are emotional obstacles to overcome, but in all things, the last two years in the mountains have helped me in all areas of my life.

'Thank you for being an amazing guide and helping me achieve this. I cannot even express in words how it has made me feel. Plus the fact that I got to share the moment with a good friend is just so special. I drove home after the In Pinn grinning from ear to ear for the whole six hour journey.'

Preparation and training

Physical fitness

The fitter you are the better, since you will be able to concentrate on the technical terrain rather than being out of breath and flustered. Any aerobic exercise is good but the more hill-specific the better.

Get out in the hills, carrying more gear than you might normally since in the Cuillin you will have a harness and helmet and may need to carry more water than usual. If your location makes hill going a challenge then get to a gym, cycle to work or do whatever is necessary to get fit. Do not underestimate the physical challenge.

Psychological fitness

For the vast majority of people who doubt their own abilities to do the Cuillin Munros, this will undoubtedly be their biggest hurdle to overcome. See Head Games.

Practice

In many ways, this overlaps with physical fitness but if you can get out and practice some of the skills, that will be helpful. Get out climbing and abseiling. Just getting used to the harness and helmet, learning to trust a rope and practicing climbing will all stand you in good stead. While plenty of people have done the Inaccessible Pinnacle as their first ever climb and abseil, those that have had some previous practice have spoken of how useful it was.

Try and get out on some of the harder mainland Munros like Liathach or the Aonach Eagach ridge, just to get some scrambling practice in and to get used to moving on rock in exposed situations.

Planning

Get the logistics sorted well in advance so you can concentrate on the important things. Decide who you are doing the Munros with (a guide or a friend), and get travel and accommodation planned.

Sgurr a' Ghreadaidh, the four Tops of Sgurr a' Mhadaidh (Route 2) and the ridge leading all the way to Sgurr nan Gillean (Route 1) at sunrise and with a temperature inversion

Strategy and tactics

Strategy and tactics will very much depend on the style you are doing the Munros in. If you are on a guided course then you will have less to think about, although a good guide should talk you through things, lay out the options and give you advice.

If you are not being guided then things are a lot more open-ended. For some people a single Munro a day will be plenty, while others may want to do three or more.

Preparation

Make sure you are ready for that first big day in the Cuillin and for the subsequent days. Eat and hydrate well, and consider having a total rest day before things kick off. Get to sleep early and try not to worry. Have all your gear checked and packed so there is no last-minute rush when the alarm goes off.

Kit list

Footwear

Keep in mind that footwear will have to serve on a variety of terrain:

- approaches on paths, grass and scree
- crossing rough terrain, scree and boulder fields
- scrambling
- rock climbing

The options are boots or approach shoes. Boots are the traditional choice and offer increased ankle support and protection, especially on scree. Approach shoes are lighter and better for the scrambling and climbing.

Whatever footwear you go for, make sure it's well worn in and works for you. The Cuillin is no place for brand-new footwear. Approach shoes are best for half decent weather and lightweight boots are best for poor conditions.

Socks are an often underrated bit of kit. Good socks will enhance your experience whereas bad socks, like bad footwear, can make your hill life miserable. Merino wool socks are great and well worth the expense.

Pack

Bring a 35–40 litre pack. Anything larger and you may well be tempted to pack too much. Any smaller and it will be a struggle to get everything in. Harness and helmet add bulk and are both best put inside the pack so they do not get damaged or lost.

Simple packs with clean exterior lines are good so they do not snag on rocks as you scramble. Use a waterproof liner to protect your kit if it rains. External waterproof covers can catch the wind and snag on rocks.

Clothing

Even in summer conditions, remember that the proximity of the Cuillin to the sea and the maritime climate can mean lots of rain, high winds and relatively low temperatures, so pack accordingly.

Even when the forecast is brilliant, take lightweight waterproofs, both jacket and trousers. With climate change, some recent summers have seen abysmal weather.

Any clothing for the Cuillin needs to be tough and durable or it will be wrecked by the gabbro. Overtrousers need at least knee-heigh zips so they can be put on/taken off without the need to remove footwear.

A spare insulated layer is always useful in case of bad weather or an emergency. A long-sleeved thermal top is good for warmth, and if you get lucky then it will also offer protection from the sun. A fleece or softshell adds a layer of warmth.

Even in summer, a hat and gloves are recommended. With the gabbro being so abrasive, a pair of leather gloves will be useful. Branded climbing gloves will do the trick but are expensive, so check out cheap gardening gloves as an alternative.

Food and drinks

A good breakfast is crucial for most people but do not neglect food during the day. Ongoing calorie intake is the fuel that will keep you going.

Be aware that opportunities to refill water bottles are very limited and plan accordingly. Water bladders and tubes encourage rehydration and are a very practical option.

To save weight it is sometimes possible to walk in part way and then fill water bottles. For the southern three Munros there is Loch Coir' a' Ghrunnda, and there are streams high in Coire a'

The approach to Bla Bheinn has fantastic views to the Munro ahead (Route 5)

The exposed moves just above where the route up Sgurr Mhic Choinnich meets Collie's Ledge (Route 3) with Bla Bheinn in the distance (Route 5)

Bhasteir. Look at maps and plan ahead but do be aware that increasing human activity and deer and sheep may mean that water is contaminated, so it makes sense to bring either a filter or purification tablets.

Walking poles

People either love or loathe poles but they can make a big difference, especially on big descents at the end of a long day. Make sure your poles pack down to a short length so they can either go inside your pack or be neatly strapped to the sides. Lots of people turn up with really heavy poles which might work well on the mainland but are a real burden when you have to carry them for scrambling.

Map

Everyone should carry their own map in case they become separated from the group. For the Cuillin, the Harvey Superwalker map is the industry standard, being large scale (1:25,000 on one side, and a super detailed 1:12,500 enlargement of the main ridge on the other).

Emergency kit

Your emergency kit should include a whistle, a bivi bag/bothy bag/survival bag, and a small first aid kit. Take a head torch even in summer, just in case you are delayed for some reason and end up descending in the dark.

Climbing gear

If you are using a guide then they will supply any technical gear like harness, helmet, sling, carabiners and abseil device. If you are going down the non-guided route then let's assume you either know what you are doing climbing-wise or are going with a skilled and experienced friend.

Your harness and especially your helmet will be worn a lot so get something that is comfortable and fairly lightweight. Even on some of the easier Munros, a helmet will offer protection from both falling rocks and from any trips or slips. A 40m rope is long enough for any of the climbs and abseils unless otherwise mentioned.

Logistics

Transport

Public transport on Skye is very limited so you'll need to either have a car or base yourself somewhere which allows access for multiple Munros, such as Glen Brittle.

There are fuel stations in Portree and Broadford.

Shops

Consider stocking up at the Co-op in Broadford when you top up with petrol. There is a larger Co-op in Portree and a small community shop in Carbost. Glen Brittle Campsite has a small shop selling essentials.

Inside Out in Portree is your best bet for any outdoor kit you have forgotten.

Pubs

Seumas' Bar at Sligachan and The Old Inn at Carbost are the closest to the Cuillin.

Accommodation

The nearer to the Cuillin the better, especially given the amount of single-track roads you will need to negotiate. Sconser, Sligachan, Crossall, Carbost, Portnalong and Glen Brittle are the closet places and offer a variety of accommodation.

There are campsites at Sligachan and Glen Brittle. The latter is ideally located and eight of the Munros can be done on foot from it. Glen Brittle Campsite also has a small shop and does fantastic coffee and croissants to kickstart your Munro day.

There is also a Youth Hostel at Glen Brittle, as well as the Glen Brittle Memorial Hut.

Geology

Skye must be a geologist's dream location. It has a wide range of rock types, and volcanicity and subsequent glaciation have sculptured a truly unique mountainscape. The Black Cuillin is composed mainly of a very rough rock, gabbro, and a finer rock, basalt, and dates from about 60 million years ago. These igneous rocks are the eroded remains of a massive volcano. The magma chamber is roughly 12km across and has been exposed by glaciation and weathering.

Gabbro is the main building block of the Black Cuillin. A very coarse-grained rock, it is typically grey, brown or black. Extremely rough, it is excellent to climb on but renowned for wearing out fingertips and footwear. Gabbro was formed from magma then cooled very slowly, deep in the earth, allowing time for crystals to grow and its rough texture to form.

Environmental considerations

Approaching the summit cairn on Sgurr nan Eag (Route 4)

Basalt is also volcanic in origin but is much smoother and finer grained. Much of the distinctive jagged shape of the Black Cuillin is due to the later intrusions of basalt through the gabbro. Basalt can be treacherous in the wet but it also facilitates ascents and descents, as the intrusions have often formed staircase-like structures.

Glaciation has shaped the Cuillin. At one stage Skye was under more than 160m of ice. During the last glacial maximum, perhaps 18,000 years ago, an ice dome was centred on the Cuillin, although much of the ridge itself may have stood clear of the ice. Lots of evidence of glaciation exists, including the glacially smoothed slabs in Coire Lagan.

Environmental considerations

With ever increasing numbers of people visiting the Cuillin, it is important to follow the principles of 'leave no trace' so as to protect this fragile environment.

Leave nothing but footprints, and take nothing but photos. Please carry all your rubbish out with you and refrain from scratching graffiti on rock or building unsightly cairns and stone stacks. Respect the wildlife and livestock, and keep dogs under close control at all times.

Use toilets before entering the Cuillin and be prepared to carry out any human waste and toilet paper. There are toilets at Glen Brittle Campsite as well as at Carbost, Sconser and Elgol.

Bla Bheinn (Route 5) with Clach Glas centre and the Corbett, Garbh-bheinn on the left

Grades

Routes on the Cuillin Munros cover a huge range of difficulty, from walking through scrambling to lower-grade rock climbs. In ascending order of difficulty, here's how the grading system works:

Grade 1 scramble

Easy scrambling. Should be fairly straightforward for experienced hillwalkers. Hands may be needed to help progress at times, but holds will be large. There could well be some exposure but nothing too scary. Descent and retreat should be easy.

Grade 2 scramble

These scrambles require a bit more thought and much more use of the hands. There may well be a lot of exposure. There may be short, quite technical sections, or the route may be less hard but difficult to escape from and retreat may well be hard. Route finding may well be more challenging.

Grade 3 scramble

The top end of the scrambling scale, this will involve harder, thought-provoking moves on steep rock in exposed positions. Many will want a rope to provide security on such terrain.

Moderate rock climb

Although the easiest climbing grade and as such should have obvious holds, there can be tricky moves and exposure can be considerable.

Difficult rock climb

Technical climbing skills will be necessary. The moves will be harder, exposed and in more serious situations.

Do keep in mind that the grades refer to the easiest line and it can be easy to get off route and onto harder terrain.

Using this guide

This guide aims to help the reader 'compleat' all the Cuillin Munros in 'summer' conditions.

This book is in two volumes; the first helps you prepare for your Munro journey, both before your arrival on Skye and after you arrive. It also has a chapter on each Munro, with background information and photos to give an idea of what to expect.

Volume two has everything necessary to actually ascend and descend the Cuillin Munros: route descriptions, maps and photo topos.

Unless you are very experienced (or being guided), it is suggested that you start with the easier Munros and build up towards the more technical ones. This will enable you to get used to the terrain, the rock types and the scale involved.

The chapters are divided as if you are doing the eleven main Cuillin Ridge Munros over four days, with Bla Bheinn as another outing. For example, day one might be the Northern Three of Sgurr nan Gillean, Am Basteir and Bruach na Frithe. If there is an easier way up one of the Munros, this will be covered separately. In this example, the west ridge will be used to ascend and descend Sgurr nan Gillean so the other two Munros can be linked in. However, the easiest route up Sgurr nan Gillean is the south-east ridge so this is covered as a separate route.

The Munro Tops are also included in the chapters for the sake of completeness.

Each chapter has a map showing numbered waypoints along the route that correlate with the numbers in the accompanying text and topos. In good visibility, the map and text may suffice. However, it is best if the map, text and photo topos are all used in conjunction.

The main route is marked in red with any alternatives in yellow. Munro Tops are marked in blue.

On the summit of Sgurr Alasdair in perfect weather (Route 4)

Munroists on flank of Sgurr nan Eag high above Coir a Ghrunnda with Sgurr Alasdair in distance (Route 4)

Any instructions such as left and right are assumed to be from the direction of travel. To avoid any confusion, sometimes additional instructions such as 'on the Glen Brittle side' or 'on the Loch Coruisk side' are added to avoid confusion.

All maps are reproduced from the Harvey Superwalker XT25 map, Skye: The Cuillin. It is recommended that you carry a hard copy of this map to provide an overview since each map section in the book only covers a limited area. A complete map also facilitates a change of plan/route should that be necessary. Many thanks to HARVEY for agreeing to the use of their maps in this guide.

GPX tracks

GPX tracks for the routes in this guidebook are available to download free at www.cicerone.co.uk/1204/GPX. If you have not bought the book through the Cicerone website, or have bought the book without opening an account, please register your purchase in your Cicerone library to access GPX and update information.

A GPS device is an excellent aid to navigation, but you should also carry a map and compass and know how to use them. GPX files are provided in good faith, but in view of the profusion of formats and devices, neither the author nor the publisher accepts responsibility for their use. We provide files in a single standard GPX format that works on most devices and systems, but you may need to convert files to your preferred format using a GPX converter such as gpsvisualizer.com or one of the many other apps and online converters available.

Higher up on the west ridge of Sgurr nan Gillean, where the terrain becomes easier and less exposed (Route 1)

The Munros

Skye Munros

Sgurr nan Eag, 924m

'peak of the notches'

The most southerly of the Munros on the Cuillin Ridge, Sgurr nan Eag involves minimal, easy scrambling and makes a good introduction to the Munros which are more than just a walk.

The approach is via Coir' a' Ghrunnda, a huge coire surrounded by mountains and a lovely loch. It's a wonderful place to stop and take in the surrounding peaks. From here, Sgurr nan Eag looks menacing, the route steep and improbable. Closer up, the ascent actually zigzags up scree and over boulders and is strenuous rather than difficult or exposed. Higher up, easy scrambling leads to the long ridge out to the summit.

Mostly fairly level, the summit ridge seems long with false summits repeatedly raising expectations. Confirmation that you are at the true summit is found with one of the largest summit cairns in the Cuillin. Rocks have been piled high to build the cairn on top of gigantic boulders. It's an impressive structure and provides a high viewpoint to not just survey the Cuillin Ridge and the outlying Munro of Bla Bheinn, but also to look out to sea and the western isles.

The first recorded ascent was by Captain J.C. Macpherson and an Ordnance Survey party in 1877.

Sgurr Dubh Mor, 944m

'big black peak'

Sgurr Dubh Mor was first climbed by Alexander Nicolson in 1873. Nicolson and an unnamed companion were walking back to Sligachan from Glen Brittle and decided to head down Glen Sligachan, their mission being to attempt the still unclimbed Sgurr Dubh Mor.

Sgurr nan Eag seen from Sgurr Sgumain (Route 4)

Sgurr Dubh an Da Bheinn

Just below the summit of Sgurr Dubh Mor and returning to Sgurr Dubh an da Bheinn. Gars-bheinn and the start of the Cuillin Ridge are in the distance and part of Sgurr nan Eag is to the right (Route 4)

The pair reached the summit at sunset and their night-time descent proved challenging, Nicolson often using his plaid as an improvised rope. His younger companion would lower Nicolson then step down onto his shoulders. At 03.00 in the morning they arrived back at Sligachan. In *The Black Cuillin* by Calum Smith, Nicolson is quoted as describing it as 'the hardest adventure I have had among those hills'.

Sgurr Dubh Mor lies to the east of the main Cuillin Ridge. The nearest peak actually on the ridge is the Munro Top Sgurr Dubh an Da Bheinn.

The scrambling is not that hard but the route is intimidating and the easiest line not necessarily that easy to find, especially in poor visibility. The terrain is continuously interesting with amazing rock formations and short steps of scrambling interspersed with easier ground.

Sgurr Dubh an Da Bheinn, 938m

By default, most Munroists will automatically bag the Munro Top of Sgurr Dubh an Da Bheinn since the easiest route between summits traverses it.

Silhouette of walker on ridge just below the summit of Sgurr Dubh an Da Bheinn, heading out to Sgurr Dubh Mor on the left (Route 4)

Sgurr Alasdair, 993m

'Alexander's peak'

Sgurr Alasdair is the highest peak on Skye and dominates the neighbouring summits. Along with the neighbouring Munro Top of Sgurr Thearlaich, it forms a distinct skyline silhouette, the Great Stone Chute a notch between them.

The first recorded ascent was by Sheriff Alexander Nicolson and Alexander MacRae in 1873. They had a good day, first ascending Sgurr na Banachdich, then continuing along to the In Pinn which (in *The Black Cuillin* by Calum Smith) Nicolson dismissed: 'It might be possible with ropes and grappling irons to overcome it but the achievement seems hardly worth the trouble.' The pair carried on, skirting below Sgurr Mhic Choinnich before ascending the Great Stone Chute to the summit of the peak where they built a cairn and celebrated with a dram.

As to the name of the peak, Nicolson suggested 'Sgurr Sgumain' which translates to 'stack', as in a haystack. The local shepherd, MacRae, pointed out that the peak below already had that name. Nicolson then suggested 'Scurr - a- Laghain' [sic] after the coire below. This never really caught on and gradually the peak came to be referred to as simply 'Alasdair', the Gaelic for Alexander. Apparently Sgurr Alasdair was previously referred to as Sgurr Biorach which translates to the brilliantly accurate 'pointed peak'.

The Great Stone Chute is the most iconic feature of the mountain and makes for the easiest ascent route. Although this is the easiest route in terms of grade, it's not easy in terms

Scrambler about to ascend the ridge from top of Stone Chute to the summit of Sgurr Alasdair. Coir' a' Ghrunnda visible far below (Route 4)

of effort. Over 300m of scree make any ascent a real challenge as you make one step up and then slide back down half a step. It is a route which succumbs to hard graft and determination.

It's a relief to reach the flat col between Sgurr Thearlaich and Sgurr Alasdair and then escape along the short, rocky ridge to the summit. The Chute used to be one of the best scree runs in the UK but repeated descents have meant all the smaller rocks have ended up near the base, leaving a mix of loose boulders and scree. There is a constant need to take care.

Should the scree approach of the Chute not appeal then the best alternative is the south-west flank via Coir' a' Ghrunnda. It's a much longer walk in but takes you to a beautiful coire with a wonderful loch. The route takes you past the Sgurr Sgumain bivi cave which offers a good shelter in poor weather before you head up the south-west flank.

The crux of the scramble is the initial chimney which looks intimidating but actually has an abundance of good holds if you search around.

Sgurr Thearlaich, 984m

'Charles' peak'

Separated from Sgurr Alasdair by the Great Stone Chute, Sgurr Thearlaich is one of the more difficult Munro Tops to reach.

First summitted in 1887 by Charles Pilkington and H. Walker, it can be combined with an ascent of Sgurr Alasdair. This is a very exposed grade 3 scramble and involves returning the same way.

Silhouetted figures approaching the summit of Sgurr Thearlaich having ascended the south ridge on the right (Route 4)

In 1895, Charles Pilkington produced his own map of 'The Cuchullin Hills', on which the Sgurr Alasdair group was subdivided into Sgurr Alasdair, Sgurr Sgumain and 'North East Peak' which later became Sgurr Thearlaich.

Sgurr Sgumain, 947m

Sgurr Sgumain is the other Munro Top close to Sgurr Alasdair and is best approached from Coir' a' Ghrunnda when it can be combined with Sgurr Alasdair, Sgurr Dubh Mor and Sgurr nan Eag.

A solitary figure below Sgurr Sgumain with Sgurr Alasdair to the right (Route 4)

Sgurr Mhic Choinnich, 948m

'Mackenzie's Peak'

Sgurr Mhic Choinnich rises from the sweeping arc of Coire Lagan. As you approach, glaciated slabs and the loch catch your eye but centre stage in the back drop is the looming bulk of Sgurr Mhic Choinnich. The bulk disguises the fact that the mountain is long and slim and access is by an increasingly narrow ridge with huge drops either side.

John Mackenzie was a well-known Cuillin guide and this peak bears the Gaelic spelling of his name, a fitting legacy for this Skye local.

Sgurr Mhic Choinnich was first ascended in 1887 by Charles Pilkington, James Heelis, Harry Walker and John Mackenzie. This team first repeated the west ridge of the In Pinn before descending around An Stac to explore a very distinctive unclimbed peak at the rear of Coire Lagan.

The team succeeded and built a summit cairn. They considered the route 'a fine easy climb with precipitous rocks on either side of the ridge' (quoted in *The Black Cuillin* by Calum Smith). By the newly built cairn, they considered what to call the peak and jokingly suggested 'Pic Mackenzie', a name that continued to be used until Pilkington's map was published in 1890 and used the Gaelic form of Sgurr Mhic Choinnich.

High on Sgurr Mhic Choinnich during a temperature inversion with the Inaccessible Pinnacle top left (Route 3)

From Coire Lagan, Sgurr Mhich Choinnich does not look particularly impressive but once you approach, its true size and bulk becomes apparent. From the bealach as you approach, Sgurr Mhic Choinnich looks formidable. An elongated wedge carved from rock, it sits high above Coire Lagan, steep cliffs protecting it.

From the top of An Stac Screes, Sgurr Mhic Choinnich looks impossible to climb. Facing you is an apparently sheer wall of rock, and the summit itself looks a long way distant with steep cliffs to each side. The route up the north ridge is a grade 2 scramble but don't underestimate it. Although it is given a relatively lowly grade, the route is long with is a lot of exposure. The rock is mainly rough gabbro but higher up there is basalt which is notoriously slippery in the wet. Despite the grade, Sgurr Mhic Choinnich is one of the hardest Munros.

The initial face is not as much of a problem as it looks. Short sections of scrambling are broken by easier scrambling and walking. After the initial steep section, the ridge levels off and the terrain makes for easier going.

The ridge is long and narrow, and higher up the drops either side become readily apparent.

The summit offers stunning views but also a reminder of the fact that you still need to descend safely. A cracked memorial stone by the summit cairn commemorates the life of a climber.

Sgurr Dearg: The Inaccessible Pinnacle, 986m

'red peak'

For many Munroists, the Inaccessible Pinnacle is the biggest barrier to their 'compleation', so it deserves more detailed coverage. This is the big one, the one all Munroists want to have in the bag although they may be dreading the actual climb. Being the most technical of all the Munros and one that involves both a graded rock climb and an abseil means it is a big challenge, but just remember that lots of Munroists have done it before you. It is achievable.

The naming is controversial since Sgurr Dearg really refers to the bulk of the mountain, the Inaccessible Pinnacle being a sheer blade of basalt on its highest flank to the east. Sgurr Dearg is 978m while the In Pinn (as it is commonly called) is 986m.

Below the In Pinn is An Stac (The Stack or Pinnacle) and it seems that in the mists of time the names have become muddled up, the In Pinn being the higher and more prominent of the two. In the 1891 edition of Munro's Tables, Sgurr Dearg is listed as a Munro with the In Pinn being relegated to a subsidiary top despite it being obviously higher. This inconsistency was remedied in the 1921 tables, a decision many nervous Munroists probably abhor.

The In Pinn was first climbed on the 18th of August 1880 by brothers Charles and Lawrence Pilkington. Some

Sgurr Dearg: The Inaccessible Pinnacle, 986m

Climber stands by the Bolster Stone on the Inaccessible Pinnacle (Route 3) with Sgurr nan Gillean to the left and Bla Bheinn to the right

credit must surely go to their unnamed local guide, although to be fair, the Pilkingtons left their guide at the base of the route while they ascended the long east ridge.

In *The Alpine Journal* volume 13, published in 1888, Charles wrote an account entitled 'The Black Coolins': 'As the mountain on which it stands also shoots away on either side, the eye seems to plunge immediately to the bottom of Glen Coruisk, 2,500ft below, giving an additional feeling of insecurity to anyone who, clinging to the narrow east ridge (on which he might be seated astride) feels the whole slab vibrate with the blow of a falling rock that he has levered out from the crest above, as actually happened on the first ascent.'

The In Pinn is a beautiful fin of rock perched high above Coire Lagan on one side and the Coruisk basin on the other. Most people approach via Sgurr Dearg's west ridge from where the In Pinn suddenly comes into view.

If the In Pinn is combined with Sgurr Mhic Choinnich then the route will involve the An Stac bypass, a series of slabs and scree.

Sgurr Dearg offers a great 360-degree view and most will leave their packs there before descending the intimidating slabs and scree to the Pinnacle.

Once at the base of the In Pinn, the climbing proper begins and is usually split into two sections or 'pitches'. Your guide or climbing partner will climb first and use the rope to secure you as you climb. The initial climbing is up a corner which is steep but, like most of the climb, it features large hand and footholds. Next, a series of stepped ledges parallel to the crest of the ridge on the Coire Lagan side are followed. These lead to a notch in the ridge which is squeezed through, and suddenly the exposure is ramped up with drops now on both sides.

Above is the crux of the climb, the hardest single section. It's only a few metres but can seem thought-provoking since footholds are small and the handholds are not as large as they have been on the climb thus far. Luckily, your guide or fellow climber will be anchored just above you. This means they are securely attached to the rock. As a bonus, they will have the rope directly above you and can keep it nice and tight to reassure you, and can perhaps even give you some physical assistance upwards as you fight gravity on the awkward moves.

After several metres, the crux is done and you will reach the belay, a small ledge roughly halfway up the climb. Time for a breather, to relax as much as possible and prepare for the second part of the climb. This is much easier than the crux but is very exposed with big drops to either side. Just take things steadily. Test each foot and handhold before committing to it. Just because the going is easier, do not get overconfident and make a mistake.

Soon, the upper part of the ridge leads to the summit of narrow slabs with the ultimate high point being the prominent Bolster Stone which juts up. Most Munroists will be happy just to be where they are, but a few may feel the need to reach up and touch the very top of the Bolster Stone. Some may want to stand on it, but remember that although it's easy to climb up, it's more awkward to descend. There will also be no rope above you protecting you should you fall and the resulting impact on the rocks below would at the very least result in serious leg injuries.

Admire the views, congratulate yourself, then focus on the descent. A stainless-steel anchor provides security for the abseil down the steep end of the In Pinn, opposite where you left your packs. Abseiling requires total faith in the gear but just remember how strong the rope and climbing gear really is.

Once back at your packs, breathe deeply and relax. The ordeal is over and you now have a grandstand seat to watch anyone else climbing the In Pinn.

The In Pinn is one of the few places in the Cuillin where things are likely to get busy and queuing for several hours is not uncommon. Go mega early or accept that you may have to wait your turn. With lots of climbers, many of whom may be worried, tempers can fray, so just be patient and try and work with everyone else who is trying to make the climb. There are worse places to be stuck in a queue!

Sgurr na Banachdich, 965m

'peak of smallpox' or 'peak of the milkmaid'

Sgurr na Banachdich is an amalgam of scree-filled corries divided by rocky ridges and leading to an easily accessed

Sgurr na Banachdich, 965m

Sgurr na Banachdaich (Route 3) seen from south ridge of Sgurr a' Ghreadaidh (Route 2)

summit. At roughly the middle of the Cuillin Ridge, it offers fantastic views in all directions. Pock-marked rocks, perhaps reminiscent of smallpox scars, may be how the peak got its name.

With three separate peaks, Sgurr na Banachdich is quite distinctive. The main summit is the Munro while the Central Top, a Munro Top, is a short distance away, 160m along the south ridge.

Although it was almost certainly ascended earlier, the first recorded ascent was in 1873 by Alexander MacRae and Alexander Nicolson. Nicolson, while exploring Coire Lagan in adverse weather, noticed a peak which he described (quoted in *The Black Cuillin* by Calum Smith) as 'one of the wildest objects I ever saw'. The next day he returned with MacRae, a local shepherd with great knowledge of the hills. The pair ascended Sgurr na Banachdich and traversed the ridge along to Sgurr Dearg and what has since become known as the 'Inaccessible Pinnacle', which he described as a 'wild beast's horn'.

Sgurr na Banachdich makes a great introduction to the Cuillin Munros. With no hands-on scrambling, it's just a walk, albeit over rough terrain and scree.

From Glen Brittle and even on the ascent, it is hard to grasp the true bulk

Scrambler on the Central Top of Sgurr na Banachdich (Route 3)

of the mountain. The initial path makes for pleasant walking but then the route goes across moorland to Coire an Eich. From here on, the route ascends scree and boulders. It's nothing technical, but it is rather arduous going.

Two Munro Tops are within easy reach of the summit. The Central Top is to the south while to the north is Sgurr Thormaid. Accessing either involves scrambling, and the terrain is a step up from the simple walk up from the Youth Hostel.

Sgurr na Banachdich's Central Top, 942m

The Central Top is about 160m south-east from the main summit. Easy scrambling down a series of rocky ledges to the right of the south ridge leads to a col just before the obvious tooth of the Central Top. Steep grade 2 scrambling on the Coire Banachdich side of it leads steeply to the summit. Return the same way, then descend to the Youth Hostel. Allow 30min for the out-and-back journey to the Central Top.

Sgurr Thormaid, 927m

Sgurr Thormaid translates as 'Norman's Peak' and is a fitting tribute to Professor Norman Collie who, along with his guide and climbing partner John Mackenzie, pioneered many of the early routes in the Cuillin.

It is a distinct pyramid shape and looks to be a fearsome climb, although it's only a grade 2 scramble. It can be accessed from either Sgurr na Banachdich or Sgurr a' Ghreadaidh.

Sgurr a' Ghreadaidh, 973m

'peak of torment or conflict'

The massive bulk of Sgurr a' Ghreadaidh is a dominant feature of the central Cuillin Ridge. It is an interesting mountain with twin summits, one a Munro and the other a Munro Top. Its north ridge is characterful with the parallel-sided chasm of Eag Dubh and the rocky protuberance of the Wart adding interest as you scramble to the summit from An Dorus. The south ridge, which links it to the neighbouring Munro Top of Sgurr Thormaid, is a beautiful arcing blade of rock.

On the 1870 Ordnance Survey® maps the peak was referred to as 'the burning peak'. There is some debate about who first ascended it. Ashley Abraham's book *Rock Climbing in Skye* names John Mackenzie and Wilberforce Newton Tribe as the first ascensionists and gives a date of 1870. If so, then this was quite a feat as their respective ages would have been 14 and 15. A more likely contender is the 1871 ascent by Matthew Forster Heddle.

The majority of Munroists will ascend Sgurr a' Ghreadaidh from An Dorus. This provides a useful introduction to the Munros which are more scrambling than walking. Sgurr a' Ghreadaidh is often combined with its neighbour, Sgurr a' Mhadaidh, which is a bit easier so it makes sense to try that first.

Both Munros are accessed from parking by Glen Brittle Youth Hostel.

Sgurr a' Ghreadaidh seen from the summit of Sgurr na Banachdich. Main summit on left, South Top on right (Route 2)

On the South Top of Sgurr a' Ghreadaidh, about to descend the south ridge. In Pinn directly above Munroist (Route 2)

The walk in passes amazing waterfalls near the start and the terrain is often lush or perhaps even wet underfoot.

The walk in is mainly on paths and is very pleasant, a gentle warm up for the ascent of the screes which lead up to An Dorus.

The crux of Sgurr a' Ghreadaidh is the steep climb out of An Dorus. It is only a few metres but in a fairly exposed position, although the rock is good with plenty of holds. Just remember that you will be returning this way and will have to down climb back into An Dorus.

Once on the summit, if conditions are kind then there are amazing views all around. Admire the scenery and chill out, then decide where to go next. Most people will probably call it a day, returning to An Dorus and then descending to the road. However, for the more adventurous, a Munro Top is within reach.

South Top of Sgurr a' Ghreadaidh, 969m

Sgurr a' Ghreadaidh's South Top is tantalisingly close, little more than a good stone's throw from the main summit. The South Top is only 3m lower and about 170m distant. However, the ridge between the two has a reputation for being narrow and exposed, with grade 3 scrambling involved.

Sgurr a' Mhadaidh, 918m

'peak of the fox'

In the 1870s, Ordnance Survey recorded Sgurr a' Mhadaidh as 'hill of the wild beast'. Occasionally a fox may be seen on the walk in to An Dorus when doing Sgurr a' Mhadaidh or its neighbour, Sgurr a' Ghreadaidh.

Sgurr a' Mhadaidh has four distinct summits and is one of the more complex parts of the Cuillin Ridge. Only the highest of its peaks is a Munro.

There is some dispute about the first ascent of this peak. Horace Walker, when applying to join the Scottish Mountaineering Club, mentioned that he had ascended Sgurr a' Mhadaidh in 1883 but at the time there seems to have been some confusion between it and the neighbouring peak, Bidein Druim nan Ramh. The first confirmed ascent was by Charles Pilkington and party in 1887.

Sgurr a' Mhadaidh is often climbed on the same day as its neighbour, Sgurr a' Ghreadaidh. Mhadaidh is the easier of the two so it makes sense to target it first. After a lovely walk up from Glen Brittle Youth Hostel, there comes the arduous scree slopes that lead up to An Dorus, a notch in the ridge. The broad scree slope becomes more defined the higher you get, the final section ascending a steep-sided gully. Simple scrambling up short steps seems a relief after the scree approach.

Sgurr a' Mhadaidh (Route 2) in winter with Bruach na Frithe in the distance to the right

The crux of the route is a few metres of scrambling up and out of An Dorus. After that, it's mainly walking interspersed with short sections of easy scrambling.

Bruach na Frithe, 958m

'slope of the deer forest'

Bruach na Frithe's summit features the only triangulation point on the whole of the Cuillin Ridge, the only other one in the mountain range being on the outlying Munro of Bla Bheinn. The fact that Bruach na Frithe is one of the most easily ascended Cuillin peaks presumably featured among the reasons for Ordnance Survey selecting it for a trig point.

The summit itself marks a huge change in direction of the Cuillin Ridge, going from north–south to east–west. Its ease of access makes it one of the most popular Cuillin peaks, and the views from it give a good idea of the convoluted nature of the Cuillin Ridge.

Doubtless it was ascended earlier, but the first recorded ascent was made by Professor Forbes and local Duncan MacIntyre in 1845. This was the same team who had previously made the first ascent of the much harder Sgurr nan Gillean.

Kevin Woods on the trig point of Bruach na Frithe during a one-day ridge traverse (Route 1)

Am Basteir, 935m

Sgurr a Fionn Choire seen from Am Basteir with Bruach na Frithe in the distance (Route 1)

The vast majority of people will take the easiest route, going past Allt Dearg, the iconic small, white house close to Sligachan, before heading up Fionn Choire to Bealach nan Lice. The east ridge then leads up to the summit of Bruach na Frithe.

The other main approach is by the north-west ridge, a grade 2 scramble. It is in a fine position with views down to the famous Fairy Pools. All the difficulties can be bypassed by scree and a path to the west.

The third ridge which leads to the summit is the south ridge which heads towards Sgurr na Bairnich and An Caisteal. This is the approach that people doing a summer Cuillin Ridge traverse would use.

Sgurr a Fionn Choire, 930m

Easy scrambling and spectacular views provide ample reward for those who summit the Munro Top of Sgurr a Fionn Choire.

Am Basteir, 935m

Traditionally said to mean 'The Executioner'. However, the meaning is obscure and may actually be 'The Baptiser'.

Am Basteir is the central peak in the classic skyline seen from Sligachan, alongside its distinctive neighbour, Bhasteir Tooth, a Munro Top. Sandwiched between Sgurr a' Bhasteir

View of Munroist approaching the summit of Am Basteir. Sgurr nan Gillean behind and right of the Munroist (Route 1)

and Sgurr nan Gillean, Am Basteir appears much smaller than Sgurr nan Gillean but is in fact only 30m lower. Sgurr a' Bhasteir appears larger due to being closer to the road.

Once you get closer, gaining height in Coire a' Bhasteir, things become much clearer and it's obvious just how big and menacing Am Basteir really is. It is a thin blade of rock balanced seemingly precariously astride the ridge. The north side of Am Basteir is plumb vertical, while the south side is just very steep.

The first recorded ascent of Am Basteir was by Hart and Mackenzie in 1887 while the neighbouring Munro Top, Bhasteir Tooth, was summited by Collie and King in the same year.

For most Munroists, the only feasible route to the summit is via the east ridge which faces towards Sgurr nan Gillean. From both Sgurr nan Gillean and Bealach a' Bhasteir, Am Basteir looks truly intimidating, much harder than the grade seems to suggest.

Most of the east ridge is walking and grade 1–2 scrambling. The exception is the so called 'Bad Step' which offers several metres of steep down climbing. This is usually given a climbing grade of Difficult and most will want

Am Basteir, 935m

Far from ideal rope technique, but this photo gives a good idea of the Bad Step on Am Basteir and how it is only a few metres high (Route 1)

the reassurance of a rope to protect it. The descent of the step is only a few metres but an unprotected fall would be a serious proposition, especially if the fall took you over the vertical northern edge of the ridge. There are anchors above the step to provide protection for the tricky moves, or they can be abseiled past.

The trouble with the Bad Step is that the footholds are incut and hard to see from above. It can be a real advantage to let somebody else go first so they can point out the holds to you. The technical climbing is literally only a few metres, and if you are protected securely by a rope from above then you can concentrate on lowering yourself down and locating the crucial footholds.

The step can be bypassed but the route around it is not that obvious and involves careful route finding, grade 2 scrambling in exposed positions, and ascending slabs with lots of loose rock.

From the summit of Am Basteir you can see the other two Northern Munros, Sgurr nan Gillean and Bruach na Frithe. The Munro Top of Bhasteir Tooth is out of sight below you but to the west and beyond it you can see a second Munro Top, Sgurr a Fionn Choire.

Skye Munros

Bhasteir Tooth is far right, showing the height loss between it and its neighbour, Am Basteir. Sgurr nan Gillean far left (Route 1)

Bhasteir Tooth, 915m

The Tooth is the most inaccessible of the Cuillin Munro Tops. With a guide or if you are experienced, it is possible to descend from the summit of Am Basteir to it, using a mixture of scrambling and abseiling. The best descent from the Tooth is via King's Cave Chimney. This involves crawling through a narrow passage into a cave followed by a steep 25m abseil.

Sgurr nan Gillean, 965m

'peak of the young men' or, more likely, 'peak of the gullies'

In many ways, Sgurr nan Gillean is the perfect mountain. With no easy route of ascent and steep drops on every side from a small summit, it looks like the stylised peak a child might draw. It also has importance as the birth place of Scottish mountaineering.

Along with Am Basteir and Sgurr a' Bhasteir, it forms the distinctive skyline seen from the road at Sligachan. This fleeting view seen by many

Sgurr nan Gillean, 965m

Sgurr nan Gillean seen from Sgurr a' Bhasteir. The west ridge is the right skyline while Pinnacle Ridge leads up to the summit from the left (Route 1)

doesn't really do justice to the complexity and beauty of the mountain.

From Sligachan, this imposing pyramid looks improbable, and was for ages considered impossible to climb. However, in 1836 Professor James Forbes, guided by local forester Duncan MacIntyre, reached the summit by the south-east ridge.

This first recorded ascent of Sgurr nan Gillean has been described as the birth of Scottish mountaineering. Forbes became an eminent geologist and glaciologist, and left his mark in the alps. He hired Duncan for ten shillings and they explored Sgurr na Stri which offered views to Sgurr nan Gillean. Duncan had previously made various attempts on Sgurr nan Gillean but always via the Coire a' Bhasteir approach.

On 7 July 1836, the duo skirted below Pinnacle Ridge and were soon on the summit after 2.5hr. Forbes described this, originally in *James David Forbes, Pioneer Scottish Glaciology* by F. Cunningham, and quoted in *The Black Cuillin* by Calum Smith. It makes for interesting reading: 'The extreme roughness of the rock rendered the ascent safe, where with any other formation it might have been considered perilous. Indeed, I have never seen a rock so adapted for clambering. At that time, I erected a cairn and temporary flag which stood, I was informed, for a whole year.'

Sgurr nan Gillean is a complex mountain with three major ridges joining to form the summit pyramid. All three ridges are classics. For a first attempt, the south-east ridge makes most sense as the easiest. If combining Sgurr nan Gillean with the other two Northern Munros, then the west ridge will provide the link. This involves airy climbing on the initial steep section and an abseil in descent. Pinnacle Ridge is a fair bit harder and involves climbing and a big abseil.

The majority of people will ascend the south-east ridge due to it being the easiest route. This is known as the 'Tourist Route' but, due to the serious and exposed scrambling involved, this is a misnomer. The lower part of the route is featureless terrain that can be confusing in less than good visibility. Higher up, the exposure increases to culminate in awkward moves above big drops where some people may want the security of a rope. The final approach to the summit is hugely exposed with steep drops to either side. More a mental than physical challenge, this sees a lot of people shuffling awkwardly or even crawling to ensure maximum contact with the rock.

The small summit is well worth all the effort involved to reach it, and has amazing views all around. Take a break on the steep-sided but surprisingly flat summit platform before contemplating the descent. The easiest way is to return down the south-east ridge, which obviously requires care and even more concentration than the ascent. People wishing to traverse the mountain, perhaps to reach Am Basteir, can descend the west ridge.

Most people going up the west ridge will be Munro baggers, intent on linking up the three Northern Munros. The west ridge is a big step up in difficulty from the south-east. The west ridge heads up from the bealach between Sgurr nan Gillean and Am Basteir and is renowned for a steep climb leading to a very exposed ridge section. The initial climb feels secure inside a gully/chimney, but once on the ridge there are big drops to either side. The crux is negotiating past the remnants of a large gendarme, or rock pillar, which collapsed in the winter of 1986/7. Above this, things ease off and much of the route is simple walking. Just below the summit, the route goes through a window in a large pinnacle.

To descend the west ridge, the steep ridge by the missing gendarme section is bypassed by an abseil. There are usually anchors in place for this.

Bla Bheinn, 928m

'blue hill'

The name derives from the Norse word *bla* and the Gaelic word *bheinn*. However, *bla* in modern Norwegian translates as blue, whereas in Old

Norse it could refer to both blue-black or black, tying in more with reality.

Bla Bheinn is one of the great mountains in the UK and often features high on popular lists. Its isolated nature, standing strong and distant from the main Cuillin Ridge, means it offers grand views in all directions.

Along with its neighbours of Clach Glas, Sgurr nan Each, Belig and Garbh-bheinn, it is considered one of the Cuillin Outliers. The outliers are geologically akin to the main Cuillin Ridge, being mainly gabbro rather than the granite of the nearby Red Cuillin. Only an accident of subsequent erosion has separated the outliers from the main Cuillin.

The first recorded ascent was in 1859 by Algernon Swinburne and John Nichol, although doubtless there were earlier ascents, not just by locals but also by tourists with guides.

The map maker, John MacCulloch, was the first to depict the Cuillin as a well-defined and crescent-shaped ridge. In a paper to the Geological Society in 1815, he wrote, 'the lofty and formidable group of the Cuchullin hills are either nameless, or only recorded in the traditional geography of the shepherds.' He only named one peak on the main ridge: Gars-bheinn. While

Bla Bheinn and Clach Glas seen from Loch Slapin (Route 5)

Clach Glas seen from the route up Bla Bheinn (Route 5)

he estimated the Cuillin to be about 3000ft high, he reckoned Bla Bheinn was even higher.

Black's Guide to Scotland, one of a series of books published by Andrew Black and published before Swinburne and Nichol's ascent, describes Bla Bheinn and advises that it should not 'be attempted without a guide, for not only is it beset with dangerous crags and precipices, but it is particularly liable to be suddenly enveloped in the mists which ascend from the lower ground and the sea.'

Approaching from Broadford, Bla Bheinn comes into view early from the B8083. As you arrive at Loch Slapin, its twin summits can often be seen in spectacular reflections on the water. Steep cliffs rise from sea level, presenting an impossible-looking route. Bla Bheinn looks impregnable to all but a climber, but the easiest route is mainly just walking, although it does involve a lot of scree and steep paths on badly eroded terrain.

Take your time and enjoy the walk. The views improve the higher you get. The summit provides unrivalled views of the main Cuillin Ridge and its eleven Munros. The Cuillin Outliers and Red Cuillin add to the view, as do vistas of Raasay with Torridon in the background, while Rum and Eigg are to the south.

Bla Bheinn, 928m

Bla Bheinn's trig point in poor conditions (Route 5)

Download the GPX files

All the routes in this guide are available for download from:

www.cicerone.co.uk/1204/GPX

as standard format GPX files. You should be able to load them into most online GPX systems and mobile devices, whether GPS or smartphone. You may need to convert the file into your preferred format using a conversion programme such as gpsvisualizer.com or one of the many other such websites and programmes.

When you follow this link, you will be asked for your email address and where you purchased the guidebook, and have the option to subscribe to the Cicerone e-newsletter.

www.cicerone.co.uk

LISTING OF CICERONE GUIDES

BRITISH ISLES CHALLENGES, COLLECTIONS AND ACTIVITIES

Great Walks on the England Coast Path
Map and Compass
The Big Rounds
The Book of the Bivvy
The Book of the Bothy
The Mountains of England and Wales
  Vol 1 — Wales
  Vol 2 — England
The National Trails
Walking the End to End Trail
Cycling Land's End to John o' Groats

LAKE DISTRICT

Bikepacking in the Lake District
Cycling in the Lake District
Joss Naylor's Lakes, Meres and Waters of the Lake District
Lake District Winter Climbs
Lake District: High Level and Fell Walks
Lake District: Low Level and Lake Walks
Mountain Biking in the Lake District
Outdoor Adventures with Children — Lake District
Scrambles in the Lake District — North
Scrambles in the Lake District — South
Trail and Fell Running in the Lake District
Walking The Cumbria Way
Walking the Lake District Fells
  — Borrowdale
  — Buttermere
  — Coniston
  — Keswick
  — Langdale
  — Mardale and the Far East
  — Patterdale
  — Wasdale
Walking the Tour of the Lake District

NORTH-WEST ENGLAND AND THE ISLE OF MAN

Walking the King Charles III England Coast Path: North West
Walking the King Charles III England Coast Path: North West
  — Cumbria Map Booklet
  — Lancashire and Merseyside Map Booklet
Cycling the Pennine Bridleway
Walking the Pennine Way
Walking the Pennine Way Map Booklet
Isle of Man Coastal Path
The Lune Valley and Howgills
Walking in Cumbria's Eden Valley
Walking in Lancashire
Walking in the Forest of Bowland and Pendle
Walking on the Isle of Man
Walking on the West Pennine Moors
Walking the Ribble Way
Hadrian's Wall Path
Hadrian's Wall Path Map Booklet

The Coast to Coast Cycle Route
The Coast to Coast Map Booklet
The Coast to Coast Walk

NORTH-EAST ENGLAND, YORKSHIRE DALES AND PENNINES

Walking the Dales Way
The Dales Way Map Booklet
Cycling the Reivers Route
Cycling the Way of the Roses
Cycling in the Yorkshire Dales
Great Mountain Days in the Pennines
Mountain Biking in the Yorkshire Dales
The Cleveland Way and the Yorkshire Wolds Way
The Cleveland Way Map Booklet
The North York Moors
Trail and Fell Running in the Yorkshire Dales
Walking in County Durham
Walking in Northumberland
Walking in Northumberland
Walking in the North Pennines
Walking in the Yorkshire Dales
  — North and East
  — South and West
Walking St Cuthbert's Way
Walking St Oswald's Way and Northumberland Coast Path

DERBYSHIRE, PEAK DISTRICT AND MIDLANDS

Cycling in the Peak District
Dark Peak Walks
Scrambles in the Dark Peak
Walking in Derbyshire
Walking in the Peak District
  — White Peak East
  — White Peak West

SOUTHERN ENGLAND

20 Classic Sportive Rides in South East England
20 Classic Sportive Rides in South West England
Bikepacking — South East Gravel
Cycling in the Cotswolds
Mountain Biking on the North Downs
South West Coast Path Map Booklet
  — Vol 1: Minehead to St Ives
  — Vol 2: St Ives to Plymouth
  — Vol 3: Plymouth to Poole
Suffolk Coast and Heath Walks
The Cotswold Way
The Cotswold Way Map Booklet
The Kennet and Avon Canal
The Lea Valley Walk
The Lea Valley Walk
The North Downs Way
North Downs Way Map Booklet
The Peddars Way and Norfolk Coast Path
The Pilgrims' Way
The Ridgeway National Trail

The Ridgeway Map Booklet
The South Downs Way
The South Downs Way Map Booklet
The Thames Path
The Thames Path Map Booklet
The Two Moors Way
Two Moors Way Map Booklet
Walking Hampshire's Test Way
Walking in Essex
Walking in Kent
Walking in London
Walking in Norfolk
Walking in the Chilterns
Walking in the Cotswolds
Walking in the Isles of Scilly
Walking in the New Forest
Walking in the North Wessex Downs
Walking on Dartmoor
Walking on Guernsey
Walking on Jersey
Walking on the Isle of Wight
Walking the Dartmoor Way
Walking the Jurassic Coast
Walking the Sarsen Way
Walking the South West Coast Path
Walks in the South Downs National Park

WALES AND WELSH BORDERS

Cycle Touring in Wales
Cycling Lon Las Cymru
Great Mountain Days in Snowdonia
Hillwalking in Shropshire
Mountain Walking in Snowdonia
Offa's Dyke Path
Offa's Dyke Map Booklet
Scrambles in Snowdonia
Snowdonia: 30 Low-level and Easy Walks
  — North
  — South
The Cambrian Way
The Pembrokeshire Coast Path
Pembrokeshire Coast Path Map Booklet
The Snowdonia Way
The Wye Valley Walk
Walking Glyndwr's Way
Walking in Carmarthenshire
Walking in Gower
Walking in Pembrokeshire
Walking in the Brecon Beacons
Walking on Gower
Walking the Severn Way
Walking the Shropshire Way
Walking the Wales Coast Path

SHORT WALKS SERIES

15 Short Walks in Dumfries and Galloway
15 Short Walks in Perthshire North — Pitlochry, Aberfeldy and Dunkeld
15 Short Walks in the Scottish Borders
15 Short Walks in the Trossachs — Callander and Aberfoyle
15 Short Walks on the Isle of Mull
15 Short Walks on the Isle of Skye

15 Short Walks on the Orkney Islands
15 Short Walks on the Shetland Islands
15 Short Walks Hadrian's Wall
15 Short Walks in the Lake District
 — Keswick, Borrowdale and Buttermere
 — Windermere Ambleside and Grasmere
 — Coniston and Langdale
15 Short Walks in Arnside and Silverdale
15 Short Walks in the Ribble Valley
15 Short Walks in Nidderdale
15 Short Walks in Northumberland — Wooler, Rothbury, Alnwick and the coast
15 Short Walks in the Yorkshire Dales
 — Grassington, Skipton, Malham and Ilkley
 — Sedbergh, Kirkby Lonsdale and Ingleton
15 Short Walks in the Peak District — Bakewell and the White Peak
15 Short Walks in the Peak District — Edale and the Hope Valley
15 Short Walks on the Malvern Hills
15 Short Walks Cheddar and the Mendips
15 Short Walks in Cornwall
 — Newquay and the North Coast
 — Falmouth and the Lizard
 — Land's End and Penzance
15 Short Walks in Norfolk — Broads and Coast
15 Short Walks in South Devon — Salcombe, Brixham and the coast
15 Short Walks in the South Downs — Brighton, Eastbourne and Arundel
15 Short Walks in the Surrey Hills
15 Short Walks on Dartmoor North — Okehampton and Chagford
15 Short Walks on Dartmoor South — Ivybridge and Princetown
15 Short Walks on Exmoor
15 Short Walks on the Isle of Wight
15 Short Walks Winchester
15 Short Walks in Bannau Brycheiniog — Brecon Beacons
15 Short Walks in Pembrokeshire — Tenby and the south
15 Short Walks in the Forest of Dean

SCOTLAND

Ben Nevis and Glen Coe
Cycling in the Hebrides
Cycling in the Hebrides
Cycling the North Coast 500
Great Mountain Days in Scotland
Mountain Biking in Southern and Central Scotland
Mountain Biking in West and North West Scotland
Not the West Highland Way: A Mountain High Way
Scotland
Scotland's Best Small Mountains
Scottish Wild Country Backpacking
Skye Munros
Skye's Cuillin Ridge Traverse
The Borders Abbeys Way
The Hebridean Way
The Hebrides
The Isle of Skye
The Skye Trail
The Southern Upland Way
The West Highland Way
West Highland Way Map Booklet
Walking Ben Lawers, Rannoch and Atholl
Walking in the Cairngorms
Walking in the Pentland Hills
Walking in the Scottish Borders
Walking in the Southern Uplands
Walking in Torridon, Fisherfield, Fannichs and An Teallach
Walking Loch Lomond and the Trossachs
Walking on Arran
Walking on Harris and Lewis
Walking on Jura, Islay and Colonsay
Walking on Mull, Coll and Tiree
Walking on Rum and the Small Isles
Walking on the Orkney and Shetland Isles
Walking on Uist and Barra
Walking Rum and the Small Isles
Walking the Cape Wrath Trail
Walking the Corbetts
 Vol 1 — South of the Great Glen
 Vol 2 — North of the Great Glen
Walking the Fife Pilgrim Way
Walking the Galloway Hills
Walking the Great Glen Way
Walking the Great Glen Way Map Booklet
Walking the John o' Groats Trail
Walking the Munros
 Vol 1 — Southern, Central and Western Highlands
 Vol 2 — Northern Highlands and the Cairngorms
Winter Climbs in the Cairngorms
Winter Climbs: Ben Nevis and Glen Coe

ALPS CROSS-BORDER ROUTES

100 Hut Walks in the Alps
Alpine Ski Mountaineering Vol 1 — Western Alps
Hiking the Tour of Monte Rosa
The Karnischer Hohenweg
The Tour of the Bernina
Trail Running — Chamonix and the Mont Blanc region
Trekking Chamonix to Zermatt
Trekking in the Alps
Trekking in the Silvretta and Ratikon Alps
Trekking Munich to Venice
Trekking the Tour du Mont Blanc
Tour du Mont Blanc Map Booklet
Walking in the Alps

FRANCE, BELGIUM AND LUXEMBOURG

Camino de Santiago — Via Podiensis
Chamonix Mountain Adventures
Cycling London to Paris
Cycling the Canal de la Garonne
Cycling the Canal du Midi
Mont Blanc Walks
Mountain Adventures in the Maurienne
Short Treks on Corsica
The GR5 Trail — Through the French Alps
The GR5 Trail — Vosges and Jura
The Moselle Cycle Route
Trekking in the Vanoise
Trekking the Cathar Way
Trekking the GR10
Trekking the GR20 Corsica
Trekking the Robert Louis Stevenson Trail
Via Ferratas of the French Alps
Walking in Provence — East
Walking in Provence — West
Walking in the Auvergne
Walking in the Brianconnais
Walking in the Dordogne
Walking in the Haute Savoie: North
Walking in the Haute Savoie: South
Walking on Corsica
Walking the Brittany Coast Path
The GR5 Trail — Benelux and Lorraine
Walking in the Ardennes
The River Loire Cycle Route
The River Rhone Cycle Route
Cycling the Route des Grandes Alpes

PYRENEES AND FRANCE/SPAIN CROSS-BORDER ROUTES

Shorter Treks in the Pyrenees
The Pyrenean Haute Route
The Pyrenees
Trekking the Cami dels Bons Homes
Trekking the GR11 Trail
Walks and Climbs in the Pyrenees

SPAIN AND PORTUGAL

Camino de Santiago: Camino Frances
Coastal Walks in Andalucia
Costa Blanca Mountain Adventures
Cycling the Camino de Santiago
Mountain Walking in Mallorca
Mountain Walking in Southern Catalunya
Spain's Sendero Historico: The GR1
The Andalucian Coast to Coast Walk
The Camino del Norte and Camino Primitivo
The Camino Ingles and Ruta do Mar
The Mountains Around Nerja
The Mountains of Ronda and Grazalema
The Sierras of Extremadura
Trekking in Mallorca
Trekking in the Canary Islands
Trekking the GR7 in Andalucia
Walking and Trekking in the Sierra Nevada
Walking in Andalucia
Walking in Catalunya — Barcelona
Walking in Catalunya — Girona Pyrenees
Walking in the Picos de Europa
Walking La Via de la Plata and Camino Sanabres
Walking on Gran Canaria
Walking on La Gomera and El Hierro
Walking on La Palma
Walking on Lanzarote and Fuerteventura

Walking on Tenerife
Walking on the Costa Blanca
Walking the Camino dos Faros
Portugal's Rota Vicentina
The Camino Portugues
Walking in Portugal
Walking in the Algarve
Walking in the Algarve
Walking on Madeira
Walking on the Azores
Cycling the Ruta Via de la Plata

SWITZERLAND

Switzerland's Jura Crest Trail
The Swiss Alps
Tour of the Jungfrau Region
Trekking the Swiss Via Alpina
Walking in Arolla and Zinal
Walking in the Bernese Oberland — Jungfrau region
Walking in the Engadine — Switzerland
Walking in Ticino
Walking in Zermatt and Saas-Fee

GERMANY

Hiking and Cycling in the Black Forest
The Danube Cycleway Vol 1
The Rhine Cycle Route
The Westweg
Walking in the Bavarian Alps
The Elbe Cycle Route

POLAND, SLOVAKIA, ROMANIA, HUNGARY AND BULGARIA

The Danube Cycleway Vol 2
The High Tatras
The Mountains of Romania

SCANDINAVIA, ICELAND AND GREENLAND

Hiking in Norway
 — North
 — South
Trekking the Kungsleden
Trekking in Greenland — The Arctic Circle Trail
Walking and Trekking in Iceland

SLOVENIA, CROATIA, SERBIA, MONTENEGRO AND ALBANIA

Hiking Slovenia's Juliana Trail
Mountain Biking in Slovenia
The Islands of Croatia
The Julian Alps of Slovenia
The Mountains of Montenegro
The Peaks of the Balkans Trail
The Slovene Mountain Trail
Walking in Slovenia: The Karavanke
Walking the Julian Alps of Slovenia
Walks and Treks in Croatia

ITALY

Alta Via 1 — Trekking in the Dolomites
Alta Via 2 — Trekking in the Dolomites
Day Walks in the Dolomites
Italy's Grande Traversata delle Alpi
Ski Touring and Snowshoeing in the Dolomites
The Way of St Francis: Via di Francesco
Trekking Gran Paradiso: Alta Via 2
Trekking in the Apennines
Trekking the Giants' Trail: Alta Via 1 through the Italian Pennine Alps
Via Ferratas of the Italian Dolomites
 — Vol 1
 — Vol 2
Walking Gran Paradiso National Park
Walking in Abruzzo
Walking in Italy's Cinque Terre
Walking in Italy's Stelvio National Park
Walking in Sicily
Walking in the Aosta Valley
Walking in the Dolomites
Walking in Tuscany
Walking in Umbria
Walking Lake Como and Maggiore
Walking Lake Garda and Iseo
Walking on the Amalfi Coast
Walking the Cammino Materano
Walking the Via Francigena Pilgrim Route
 — Part 1
 — Part 2
 — Part 3
 — Part 4
Walks and Treks in the Maritime Alps

IRELAND

The Wild Atlantic Way and Western Ireland
Walking the Kerry Way
Walking the Wicklow Way

INTERNATIONAL CHALLENGES, COLLECTIONS AND ACTIVITIES

Europe's High Points
Pocket First Aid and Wilderness Medicine

AUSTRIA

Innsbruck Mountain Adventures
Trekking Austria's Adlerweg
Trekking in Austria's Hohe Tauern
Trekking in Austria's Stubai Alps
Trekking in Austria's Zillertal Alps
Walking in Austria
Walking in the Salzkammergut: the Austrian Lake District

MEDITERRANEAN

Trekking in Greece
Walking and Trekking in Zagori
Walking and Trekking on Corfu
Walking on the Greek Islands — the Cyclades
Walking in Cyprus
Walking on Malta

HIMALAYA

8000 metres
Annapurna
Everest: A Trekker's Guide
Trekking in the Indian Himalayas
Trekking in the Karakoram

NORTH AMERICA

Hiking and Cycling the California Missions Trail
Hiking the Pacific Crest Trail
The John Muir Trail

SOUTH AMERICA

Aconcagua and the Southern Andes
Hiking and Biking Peru's Inca Trails
Trekking in Torres del Paine

AFRICA

Climbing Toubkal
Kilimanjaro
Walking in the Drakensberg
Walks and Scrambles in the Moroccan Anti-Atlas

NEW ZEALAND AND AUSTRALIA

Hiking the Overland Track

CHINA, JAPAN AND ASIA

Hiking and Trekking in the Japan Alps and Mount Fuji
Hiking in Hong Kong
Japan's Kumano Kodo Pilgrimage
Trekking in Bhutan
Trekking in Ladakh
Trekking in Tajikistan
Trekking in the Himalaya

TECHNIQUES

Fastpacking
The Mountain Hut Book

MINI GUIDES

Alpine Flowers
Navigation

MOUNTAIN LITERATURE

A Walk in the Clouds
Abode of the Gods
Fifty Years of Adventure
The Pennine Way — the Path, the People, the Journey
Unjustifiable Risk?

For full information on all our guides, books and eBooks,
visit our website:
www.cicerone.co.uk

CICERONE

Trust Cicerone to guide your next adventure, wherever it may be around the world...

Discover guides for hiking, mountain walking, backpacking, trekking, trail running, cycling and mountain biking, ski touring, climbing and scrambling in Britain, Europe and worldwide.

Connect with Cicerone online and find inspiration.

- buy books and ebooks
- articles, advice and trip reports
- GPX files and updates
- regular newsletter

cicerone.co.uk

Skye Munros Topo booklet

Detailed topo booklet to all the Cuillin Munros

by Adrian Trendall

JUNIPER HOUSE, MURLEY MOSS,
OXENHOLME ROAD, KENDAL, CUMBRIA LA9 7RL
www.cicerone.co.uk

© Adrian Trendall 2026
First edition 2026
ISBN: 978 1 78631 320 1
eISBN: 978 1 78765 236 1

Cicerone's EU representative for GPSR compliance is Easy Access System Europe, Mustamäe tee 50, 10621 Tallinn, Estonia. Email gpsr.requests@easproject.com.

Printed in China on responsibly sourced paper on behalf of Latitude Press Ltd.
A catalogue record for this book is available from the British Library.
All photographs are by the author unless otherwise stated.

Maps are reproduced with permission from HARVEY Maps, www.harveymaps.co.uk

> ### Updates to this guide
>
> While every effort is made by our authors to ensure the accuracy of guidebooks as they go to print, changes can occur during the lifetime of an edition. Any updates that we know of for this guide will be on the Cicerone website (www.cicerone.co.uk/1204/updates), so please check before planning your trip. We also advise that you check information about such things as transport, accommodation and shops locally. Even rights of way can be altered over time. We are always grateful for information about any discrepancies between a guidebook and the facts on the ground, sent by email to updates@cicerone.co.uk.
>
> **Register your book:** To sign up to receive free updates, special offers and GPX files where available, create a Cicerone account and register your purchase via the 'My Account' tab at www.cicerone.co.uk.

Front cover: An Stac Bypass as seen from Sgurr Mhic Choinnich (Route 3)

Contents

Route summary table 5
Map key 5

INTRODUCTION 7
Using this guide 7

THE CUILLIN MUNRO ROUTES 9

Route 1   **The Northern Three Munros** 10
          Approach to Bealach a' Bhasteir 14
          Sgurr nan Gillean 16
          Am Basteir 19
          Bhasteir Tooth via the Bhasteir Nick 22
          Bruach na Frithe 23
          Sgurr a Fionn Choire 25
          Bruach na Frithe via Fionn Choire 25
          Sgurr nan Gillean via the south-east ridge 27

Route 2   **The Central Two Munros** 36
          Approach to An Dorus 38
          Sgurr a' Mhadaidh 41
          Sgurr a' Ghreadaidh 44
          Sgurr a' Ghreadaidh's South Top and Sgurr Thormaid (and Sgurr na
          Banachdich) 47

Route 3   **The South Central Three Munros** 51
          Approach to Coire Lagan 54
          Sgurr Mhic Choinnich 56
          Linking Sgurr Mhic Choinnich and the Inaccessible Pinnacle 62
          The Inaccessible Pinnacle 64
          Sgurr Dearg to Sgurr na Banachdich 69
          Sgurr Thormaid 72
          Descent from Sgurr na Banachdich 72
          Sgurr Dearg/The Inaccessible Pinnacle via Sgurr Dearg's west ridge .. 75

Route 4	**The Southern Three Munros** 80
	Approach to Coir' a' Ghrunnda 82
	Sgurr nan Eag 86
	Sgurr Dubh Mor via Sgurr Dubh an Da Bheinn 89
	Sgurr Dubh an Da Bheinn to Sgurr Alasdair 94
	Sgurr Sgumain 99
	Sgurr Thearlaich 100
	Sgurr Alasdair via the Great Stone Chute and south-east ridge 102
Route 5	**Bla Bheinn and the South Top** 105

Warning! Climbing and scrambling can be dangerous

Climbing and scrambling can be dangerous activities carrying a risk of personal injury or death. It should be undertaken only by those with a full understanding of the risks and with the training and experience to evaluate them. Mountaineers should be appropriately equipped for the routes undertaken. Whilst every care and effort has been taken in the preparation of this book, the user should be aware that conditions are highly variable and can change quickly. Holds may become loose or fall off, rockfall can affect the character of the route, and in winter, snow and avalanche conditions must be carefully considered. These can materially affect the seriousness of a scramble, tour or expedition.

Therefore, except for any liability which cannot be excluded by law, neither Cicerone nor the author accept liability for damage of any nature including damage to property, personal injury or death arising directly or indirectly from the information in this book.

Route summary table

Route Number	Name	Start/finish	Time	Distance	Ascent	Grade	Page
1	Northern 3	Sligachan	7–9hr	14km	1350m	Climbing to Difficult	10
2	Central 2	Glen Brittle Youth Hostel	6–7hr	9km	1000m	Grade 3 scrambling	36
3	South Central 3	Glen Brittle Campsite	8–9hr	12km	1400m	Moderate climbing	51
4	Southern 3	Glen Brittle Campsite	9–11hr	12.5km	1450m	Grade 3 scrambling	80
5	Bla Bheinn	JMT car park, Loch Slapin	4–5hr	8.5km	919m	Walk	105

Symbols used on maps and topos

 route

 alternative route

 Munro top

 start point

 finish point

 start/finish point

 route direction

 numbered waymark (main route)

 numbered waymark (alt route)

 lettered waymark (munro top)

GPX files for all routes can be downloaded free at
www.cicerone.co.uk/1204/GPX

Climber about to exit the initial chimney pitch on the south-west flank of Sgurr Alasdair (Route 4)

Introduction

Using this guide

This guide aims to help the reader 'compleat' all the Cuillin Munros in 'summer' conditions.

This book is in two volumes; the first helps you prepare for your Munro journey, both before your arrival on Skye and after you arrive. It also has a chapter on each Munro, with background information and photos to give an idea of what to expect.

Volume two has everything necessary to actually ascend and descend the Cuillin Munros: route descriptions, maps and photo topos.

Unless you are very experienced (or being guided), it is suggested that you start with the easier Munros and build up towards the more technical ones. This will enable you to get used to the terrain, the rock types and the scale involved.

The chapters are divided as if you are doing the eleven main Cuillin Ridge Munros over four days, with Bla Bheinn as another outing. For example, day one might be the Northern Three of Sgurr nan Gillean, Am Basteir and Bruach na Frithe. If there is an easier way up one of the Munros, this will be covered separately. In this example, the west ridge will be used to ascend and descend Sgurr nan Gillean so the other two Munros can be linked in. However, the easiest route up Sgurr nan Gillean is the south-east ridge so this is covered as a separate route.

The Munro Tops are also included in the chapters for the sake of completeness.

Each chapter has a map showing numbered waypoints along the route that correlate with the numbers in the accompanying text and topos. In good visibility, the map and text may suffice. However, it is best if the map, text and photo topos are all used in conjunction.

The main route is marked in red with any alternatives in yellow. Munro Tops are marked in blue.

Any instructions such as left and right are assumed to be from the direction of travel. To avoid any confusion, sometimes additional instructions such as 'on the Glen Brittle side' or 'on the Loch Coruisk side' are added to avoid confusion.

All maps are reproduced from the Harvey Superwalker XT25 map, Skye: The Cuillin. It is recommended that you carry a hard copy of this map to provide an overview since each map section in the book only covers a limited area. A complete map also facilitates a change of plan/route should that be necessary. Many thanks to HARVEY Maps for agreeing to the use of their maps in this guide.

The Inaccessible Pinnacle seen from where you leave your packs (Route 3). Sgurr Alasdair and The Great Stone Chute to the right (Route 4)

GPX tracks

GPX tracks for the routes in this guidebook are available to download free at www.cicerone.co.uk/1204/GPX. If you have not bought the book through the Cicerone website, or have bought the book without opening an account, please register your purchase in your Cicerone library to access GPX and update information.

A GPS device is an excellent aid to navigation, but you should also carry a map and compass and know how to use them. GPX files are provided in good faith, but in view of the profusion of formats and devices, neither the author nor the publisher accepts responsibility for their use. We provide files in a single standard GPX format that works on most devices and systems, but you may need to convert files to your preferred format using a GPX converter such as gpsvisualizer.com or one of the many other apps and online converters available.

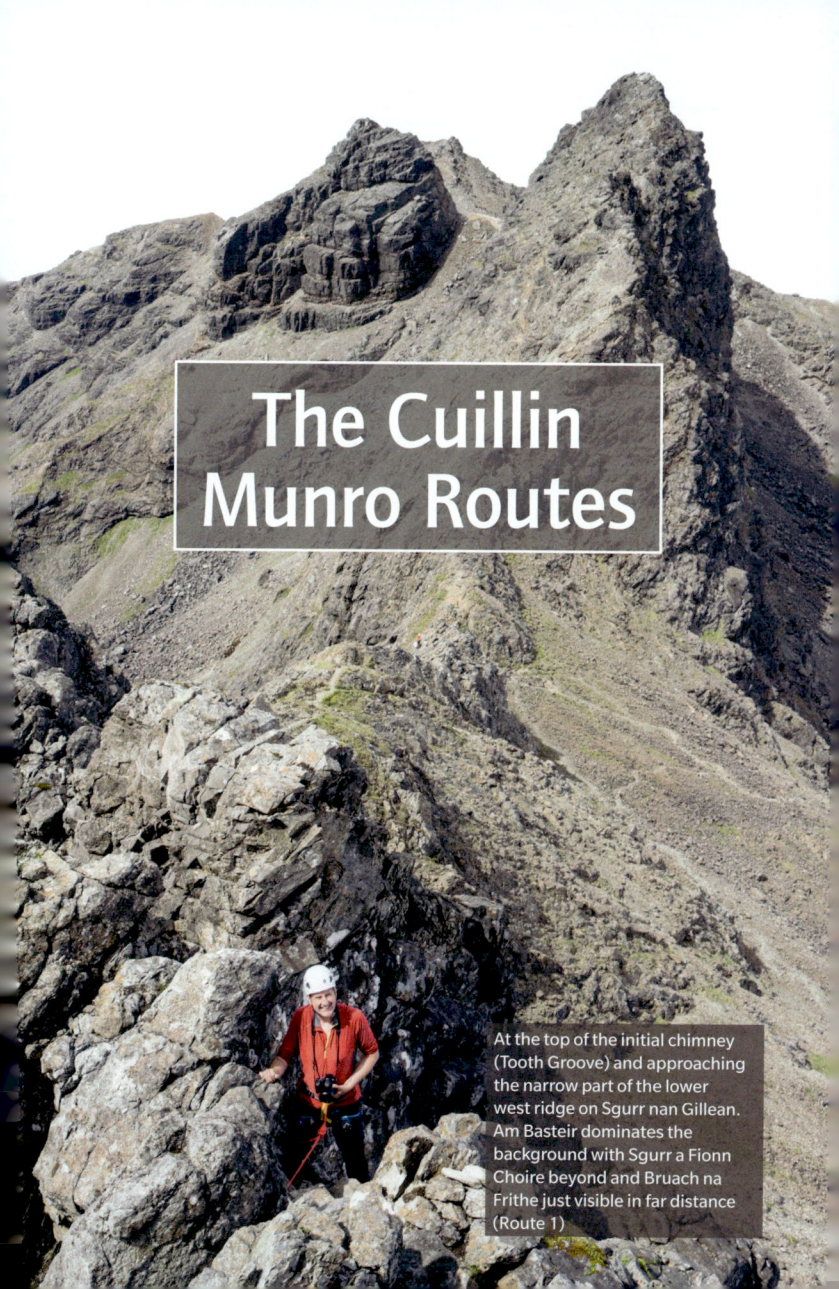

The Cuillin Munro Routes

At the top of the initial chimney (Tooth Groove) and approaching the narrow part of the lower west ridge on Sgurr nan Gillean. Am Basteir dominates the background with Sgurr a Fionn Choire beyond and Bruach na Frithe just visible in far distance (Route 1)

Route 1
The Northern Three Munros

Sgurr nan Gillean

Am Basteir

Bruach na Frithe

(+ Munro Tops, Sgurr a Fionn Choire and Bhasteir Tooth)

(+ Sgurr nan Gillean via the easiest route: the south-east ridge)

Start/finish	NG 484 298. Layby next to Skye Mountain Rescue Team base at Sligachan on the A863
Time	7–9hr
Distance	14km
Total ascent/descent	1350m
Grade	Scrambling and climbing to Moderate/Difficult
Warning	Am Basteir is basalt and can be treacherously slippery in the wet. The Bealach a' Bhasteir ravens are adept at breaking into backpacks in search of food.

Climbs the iconic skyline as seen from Sligachan and covers technical terrain involving climbing and an abseil. A physically and mentally demanding day with graded rock climbs on Sgurr nan Gillean and Am Basteir, followed by rough walking to Bruach na Frithe.

Sgurr nan Gillean and Am Basteir are much harder than Bruach na Frithe so it is best to do these first while still full of energy.

Note that there are easier routes to ascend Sgurr nan Gillean (via the south-east ridge) and Bruach na Frithe (via Fionn Choire), and these are covered later in the chapter.

The walk in to Fionn Choire from Allt Dearg passes beautiful streams with views to the Red Cuillin

Guided group approaching Sgurr nan Gillean summit having just gone through the window in the pinnacle on the West Ridge

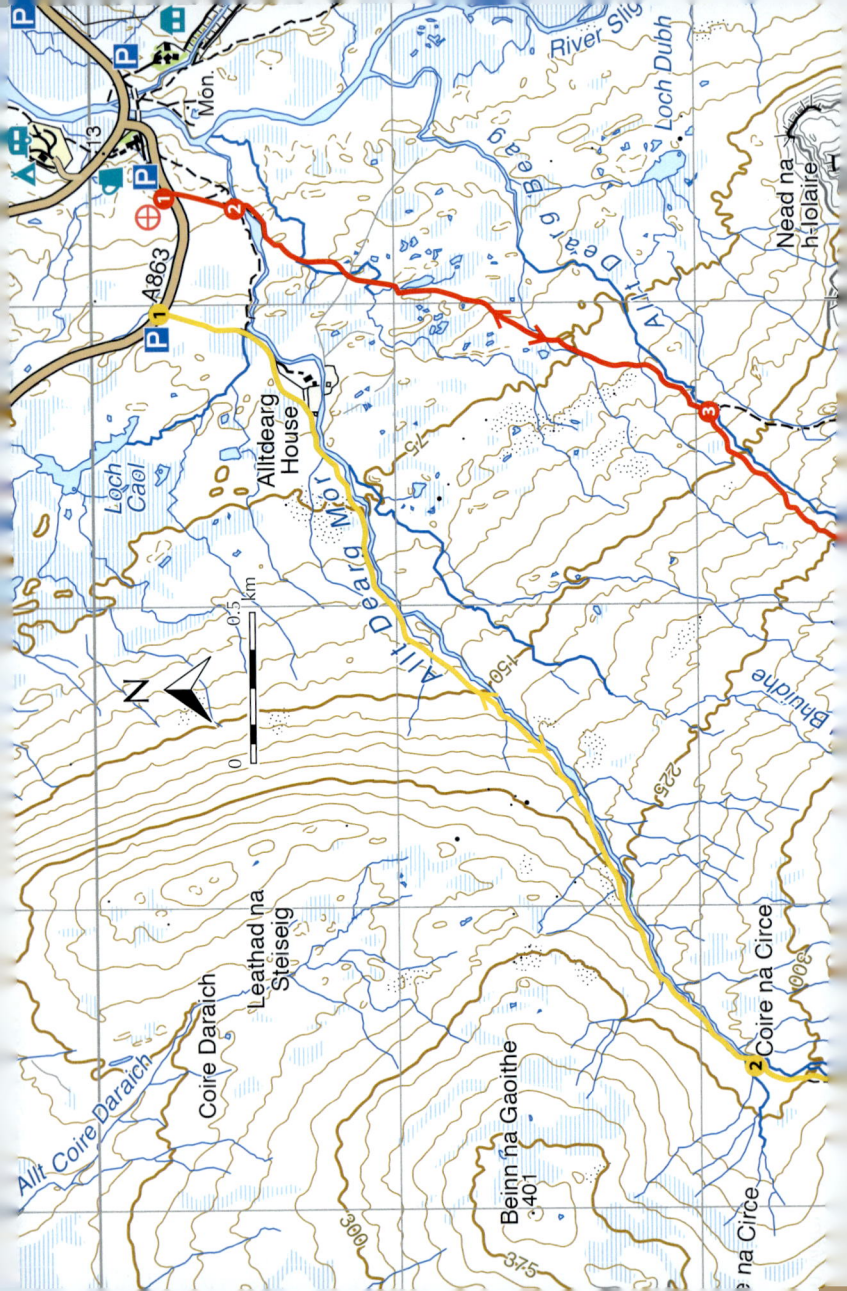

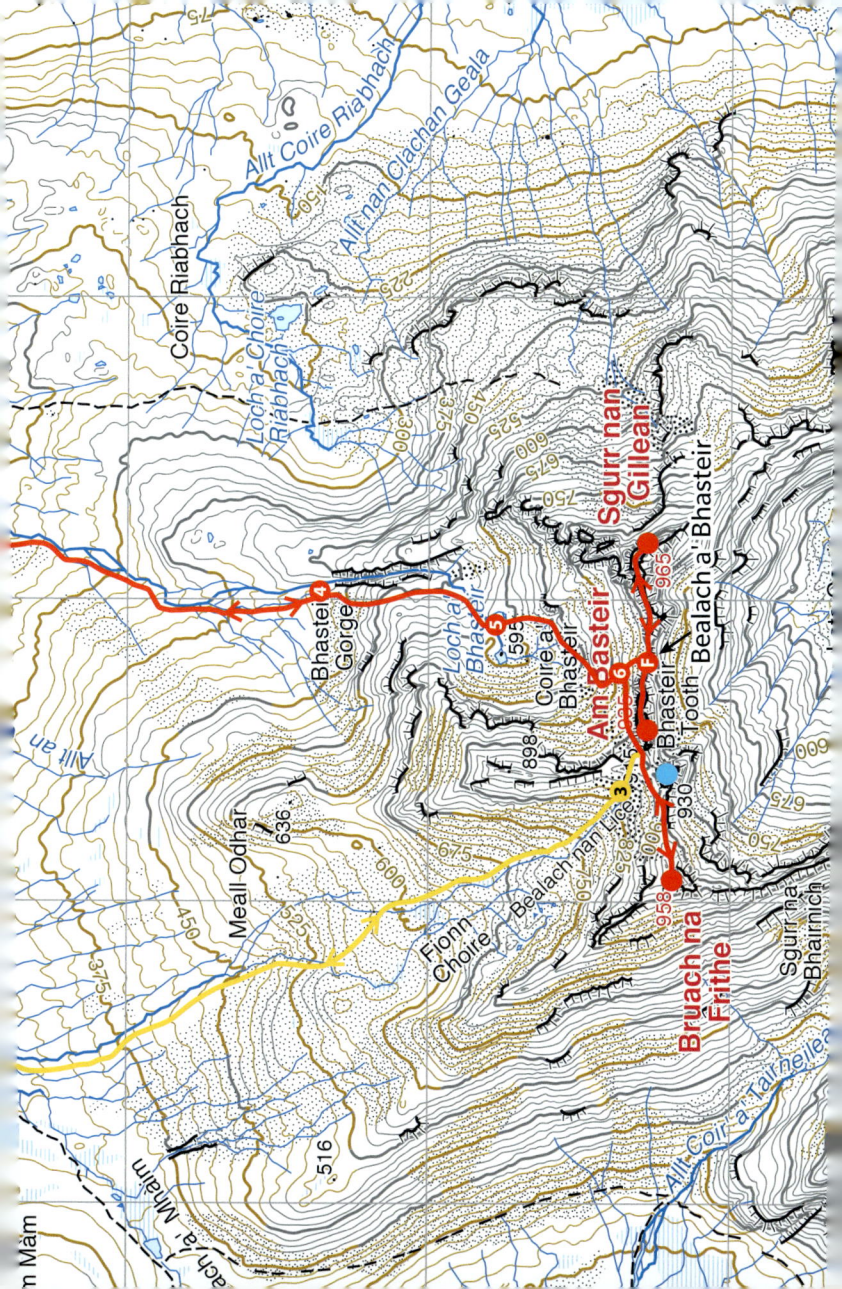

Approach to Bealach a' Bhasteir

Start/finish	NG 484 298. Layby next to Skye Mountain Rescue Team base at Sligachan on the A863
Time	2hr
Distance	5.5km
Total ascent/descent	785m
Grade	Rough walking with some very easy scrambling up to the side of Bhasteir Gorge
Warning	Some of the streams below Bhasteir Gorge can become difficult or impossible to cross if in spate

A beautiful walk with the Black Cuillin ahead and the Red Cuillin to the left as you follow streams up past Bhasteir Gorge and into Coire a' Bhasteir. Scree then leads up to Bealach a' Bhasteir.

❶ Park at the layby next to Skye Mountain Rescue base just east of the Sligachan Hotel on the A863 (NG 484 298). Please keep the entrance to the Rescue base clear of cars.

Cross the road and head towards the Cuillin on a good path.

❷ Cross the river by a narrow footbridge then continue on a good path.

❸ A second footbridge is ignored. Continue to the right on the west bank of **Allt Dearg Beag**, heading towards Coire a' Bhasteir.

❹ Ahead, the formidable entrance to Bhasteir Gorge and the shoulder of Sgurr a' Bhasteir block entry to Coire a' Bhasteir. Zigzag up scree right of the gorge then scramble up slabs and rocky steps to reach a path which contours round to the stream flowing out of **Loch a' Bhasteir**.

❺ Cross the stream (possible water source) and cross grass and rocks to pick up a path which zigzags up screes below Am Basteir.

❻ Now it's decision time. For Bruach na Frithe, head right and follow the scree under the towering bulk of Am Basteir. For Sgurr nan Gillean and Am Basteir, head up and left to reach **Bealach a' Bhasteir**, the col between Am Basteir and Sgurr nan Gillean.

It is possible to leave packs at Bealach a' Bhasteir and make out-and-back trips to **Am Basteir** and **Sgurr nan Gillean** if you judge conditions to be suitable. Be aware that the local ravens are very adept at getting into packs to access any food.

Skye Munros Topo Booklet

Sgurr nan Gillean

Route	West ridge
Grade	Climbing grade of Moderate and an abseil descent
Peak height	965m

Sgurr nan Gillean is one of the most beautiful peaks in the Cuillin and has no easy route of ascent. The route up the west ridge starts off with a graded rock climb and an exposed traverse with easier terrain leading to the small summit.

❶ From Bealach a' Bhasteir, head east towards Sgurr nan Gillean. Easy scrambling and a path leads to the base of the ridge.

❷ Scramble up a corner/gully.

❸ Climb over some boulders to follow a horizontal ledge/path left of the ridge to reach the base of **Tooth Groove** (Moderate). If you reach a large recess with an obvious chimney then you have gone about 5m too far.

❹ Two boulders mark the base of the route. A series of steps in the groove leads to the arête. Cross to the other side of the ridge then head along the ridge in a very exposed position. The pinnacle is taken to the left by a tricky move to reach a gap in the ridge, then climb up on good holds to reach the belay at the top of **Tooth Chimney**. There is an in situ anchor which will be used for the abseil when returning.

The rest of the ridge is much easier, much of it just walking with nothing harder than a grade 2 scramble although it's fairly exposed in places.

Climb a short corner above the abseil point to reach a path and then sections of short easy scrambling up and left.

❺ Zigzag up past **Top Knot Pinnacle** with its distinctive perched boulder.

❻ An exposed section up a steep rib leads up to the **Window Pinnacle** just below the summit.

❼ Go through the window in the pinnacle then head up a corner on the left to reach the ridge leading to the summit. The last section to the summit is best taken on the left of the ridge with a short step leading up to the summit of **Sgurr nan Gillean** and a cairn.

Descent: Return down the west ridge. This is mostly easy scrambling but do err on the side of caution and use a rope if in any doubt. Return to the in situ abseil anchor at the top of Tooth Chimney.

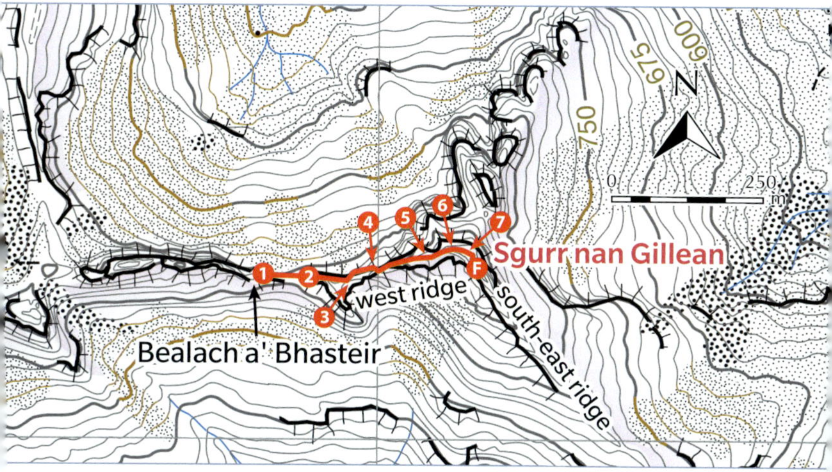

Route 1 – The Northern Three Munros

For safety, a 50m rope is advised for the abseil descent of Tooth Chimney. It can be done with a 40m rope (or shorter) but this will involve down scrambling the bottom part unprotected by a rope.

Return to **Bealach a' Bhasteir**.

Going through a window in a large pinnacle just below the summit on the west ridge, Sgurr nan Gillean

Route 1 – The Northern Three Munros

Am Basteir

Route	East ridge
Grade	Climbing grade of Difficult (or grade 2 scrambling if taking the bypass)
Peak height	935m

From Bealach a' Bhasteir, Am Basteir looks intimidating, but most of the east ridge is easy scrambling. The major difficulties of the Bad Step are confined to a few metres of down climbing.

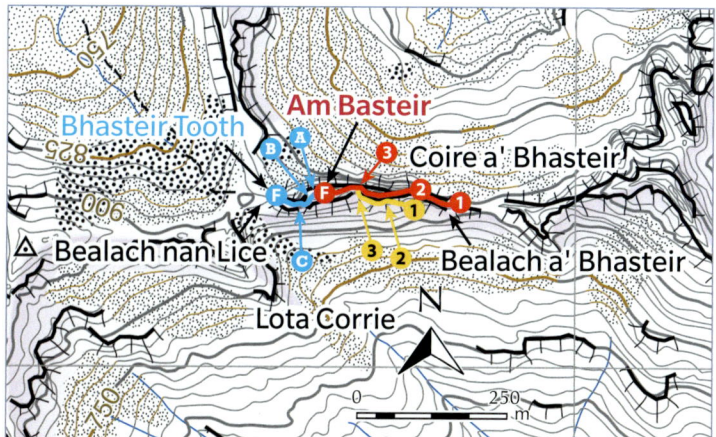

❶ Leave Bealach a' Bhasteir and head west towards Am Basteir. Scramble up rocks at the end of the bealach, taking them on the left, then turn back immediately right to follow the well-worn rocks towards the crest of the ridge.

Follow easy-angled slabs. As height is gained, a view opens up back down to Bealach a' Bhasteir.

❷ Traverse left and upwards via slabs and ramps beneath two small pinnacles on the actual crest. The crest can be taken direct but it is easier and less exposed to traverse on the left side. At the end of the ledges descend a steep corner to a brown slab which is followed up to the crest, then go along and down a short step to the Bad Step.

Route 1 – The Northern Three Munros

❸ The Bad Step is only a few metres and graded Difficult, for just a couple of moves of down climbing but in a very exposed position where you definitely wouldn't want to fall. There are good footholds but they are incut and hard to see from above so send the best climber down first so they can point out the footholds to the others. It may only be a few metres of descent but given the incut nature of the holds and the undercut base, it is very daunting.

Just before you get to the Bad Step there are anchors that can be used to protect the down climb. Given the potential seriousness of a fall, it is strongly recommended that a rope is used.

From below the Bad Step it is an easy scramble to the summit of **Am Basteir**.

Descent: Unless you are bagging the Munro Top of Bhasteir Tooth, retrace the route to **Bealach a' Bhasteir**. The Bad Step is much easier in ascent so the return journey may seem anticlimactic.

Far from ideal rope technique, but this photo gives a good idea of the Bad Step on Am Basteir and how it is only a few metres high

Grade 2 scrambling alternative to the Bad Step

> Note that although this may seem an easy alternative as a grade 2 scramble, it is very exposed, the route is not obvious, and there's a lot of loose rocks on potentially slippery slabs. As for the Bad Step, head up the initial ridge from the bealach.

1 Leave the ridge to follow traces of a path to the left. Follow this south and reach an orange/brown slab.

2 Partially ascend the slab for about 7m then turn horizontally to the left and follow a rocky ramp. Carry on around with a lot of exposure, and traverse a wall to reach a purple ramp.

3 The ramp leads up to reach the crest just past the Bad Step.

Bhasteir Tooth via the Bhasteir Nick

Route	Am Basteir–Bhasteir Tooth Link
Grade	Grade 3 scrambling and abseil
Peak height	915m

> Bhasteir Tooth is the most inaccessible of the Cuillin Munro Tops. The easiest and most convenient route is to combine it with the summit of Am Basteir. This is only covered briefly since it is assumed that anyone doing this will be either an experienced climber or being guided.

See Am Basteir map and topo.

In ascent, this route involves climbing to at least Very Difficult grade but in descent, most parties will abseil. There are usually abseil anchors in situ.

Scramble down from Am Basteir's summit to (usually in situ) abseil anchors.

A From the anchors abseil down steep terrain to slabs.

B Scramble (or abseil) down to the **Bhasteir Nick**, the obvious gap between Am Basteir and Bhasteir Tooth.

C A rib then a slab leads up to the summit of **Bhasteir Tooth**.

Route 1 – The Northern Three Munros

Descent: Return to the Bhasteir Nick where the easiest option is to descend King's Cave Chimney. This involves a 25m abseil from a cave which is reached by a squirm through a tunnel from the Bhasteir Nick.

Bruach na Frithe

Route	East ridge
Grade	Rough walking
Peak height	958m

Bruach na Frithe is simple to add on, being just a short walk after the technical terrain of Sgurr nan Gillean and Am Basteir.

1 From Bealach a' Bhasteir, retrace your original route and follow the path down scree to where the path forks. The right fork takes you back down into Coire a' Bhasteir and the left leads up scree and boulders below Am Basteir and out to Bruach na Frithe. The out-and-back to Bruach na Frithe is a straightforward walk with only minimal easy scrambling. If conditions dictate then consider leaving packs at the path junction to retrieve on your return.

Scree leads up to **Bealach nan Lice**.

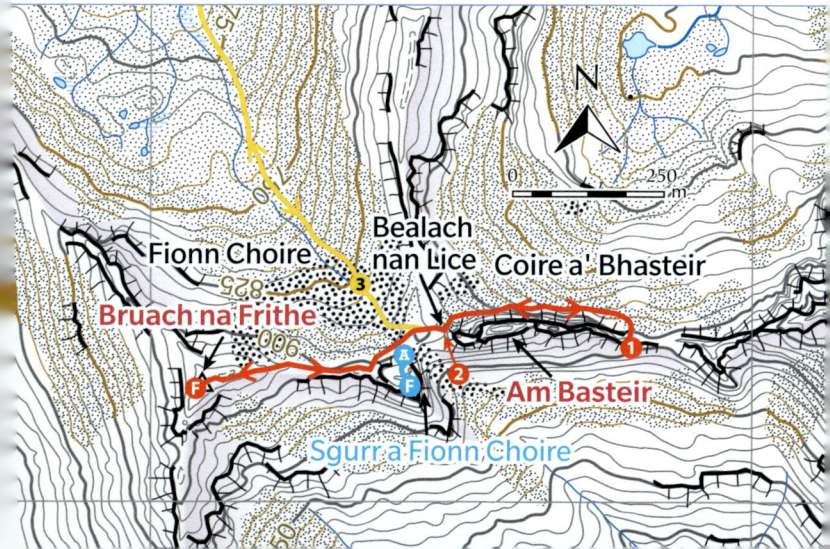

Route 1 – The Northern Three Munros

2 Bealach nan Lice offers great views across to Bla Bheinn sandwiched between two Munro Tops. To your left is Bhasteir Tooth and on the right is Sgurr a Fionn Choire. Follow faint signs of a path across scree below Sgurr a Fionn Choire, then the easiest line follows slight signs of a path below the actual ridge line on the Lota Coire (south) side. If you stick to the ridge, there is a bit of easy scrambling to reach the summit of **Bruach na Frithe**.

Descent: Return to Bealach nan Lice then descend back into **Coire a' Bhasteir**. Walk out to Sligachan.

Sgurr a Fionn Choire

Route	Central Gully
Grade	Grade 1
Peak height	915m

Sgurr a Fionn Choire is a Munro Top and easily accessed when bagging Bruach na Frithe. Start from Bealach nan Lice.

A See Bruach na Frithe map and topo **B**.

C The easiest route is via the Central Gully. This obvious gully splits the north face and is a grade 1 scramble to the summit of **Sgurr a Fionn Choire**.

The west ridge, facing Bruach na Frithe, is harder at a grade 2/3 scramble.

Bruach na Frithe via Fionn Choire

Start/finish	NG 479 297 on the A863
Time	5–7hr
Distance	13.75km
Total ascent/descent	947m
Grade	Rough walking
Peak height	958m
Warning	After heavy rainfall the streams/rivers may be in spate and difficult to cross, especially Allt Dearg Mor.

Bruach na Frithe boasts the only trig point on the entire Cuillin Ridge

This route is easier than the Coire a' Bhasteir route and makes a great introduction to the Cuillin Munros. It covers some rough terrain, scree and boulders, but there is no real scrambling involved.

See Route 1 overview map.

1 The best place to park is the small layby by the access track to Alltdearg, the small white house about 700m west of The Sligachan Hotel on the A863.

Walk up the track almost as far as Alltdearg House but turn right along a signposted path.

Follow the path alongside the **Allt Dearg Mor** to **Coire na Circe**, going past some of the best waterfalls and pools on Skye. The path splits by a small cairn. Take the left fork.

2 Cross the Allt Dearg Mor and follow the path on the west bank of Allt an Fionn Choire. If there has been a lot of rain then this river crossing can be problematic.

Cross the Allt an Fionn Choire then head across boggy grassland and scree before ascending to the left of the stream coming out of the upper coire.

3 Just below the final scree slopes, there is a spring surrounded by vivid green mosses. This is a good spot to refill water bottles. Zigzag up screes to reach **Bealach nan Lice**.

From Bealach nan Lice, head right and skirt beneath Sgurr a Fionn Choire, then the easiest line follows slight signs of a path below the actual ridge line on the Lota Coire side. If you stick to the ridge, the route involves a bit of easy scrambling.

Arrive at the summit of **Bruach na Frithe** with the only trig point on the whole of the Cuillin Ridge.

Descent: Return to Bealach nan Lice, drop into Fionn Choire and retrace your outward route.

Route 1 – The Northern Three Munros

Sgurr nan Gillean via the south-east ridge

Start/finish	NG 484 298. Layby next to Skye Mountain Rescue base at Sligachan on the A863
Time	5–7hr
Distance	12km
Total ascent/descent	980m
Grade	Grade 2/3
Peak height	965m
Warning	Very exposed on the final part of the ridge
	Navigation can be confusing, especially in upper Coire Riabhach

The south-east ridge is the easiest route up this beautiful mountain but do not underestimate the challenge. The route is sometimes called the Tourist Route, but this is a misnomer since there is some very exposed scrambling for which some people may require the security of a rope. In addition, the lower approaches are rugged and featureless, making navigation a challenge in conditions which are any less than ideal. Higher up the terrain is steep and exposed and the easiest line is not always obvious. The crux moves are high up and involve awkward moves in very exposed positions, requiring a combination of both physical and mental skills. The upper part of the ridge is complex. At all times, it must be remembered that this will be the easiest line of descent, so keep that in mind as you ascend.

In light of the above warning, do not be put off but be prepared and ready to meet the challenge. Choose a day with a good forecast, and don't hesitate to carry a rope with you and use it if necessary.

Having ascended the south-east ridge, two scramblers pause just below the summit of Sgurr nan Gillean. Bla Bheinn is in the background

Skye Munros Topo Booklet

1 Park at the layby (NG 484 296), cross the A863 and then take the footpath to a wooden footbridge which allows you to cross the **Allt Dearg Mor**. Continue on a good path to a second bridge.

2 Cross the airy bridge which consists of two planks and no rails. Continue along the path and ascend to a large cairn.

3 At the large cairn, continue ahead on the path. (A path to the right leads to the base of Pinnacle Ridge.) The path descends into lower Coire Riabhach with **Loch a' Choire Riabhach** to your left. The path then zig-zags up scree and rocks leading to middle Coire Rhibhach. The path becomes less distinct as you cross the coire. At the far end of the coire a stream descends from a series of slabs and scree below Sgurr nan Gillean's east face.

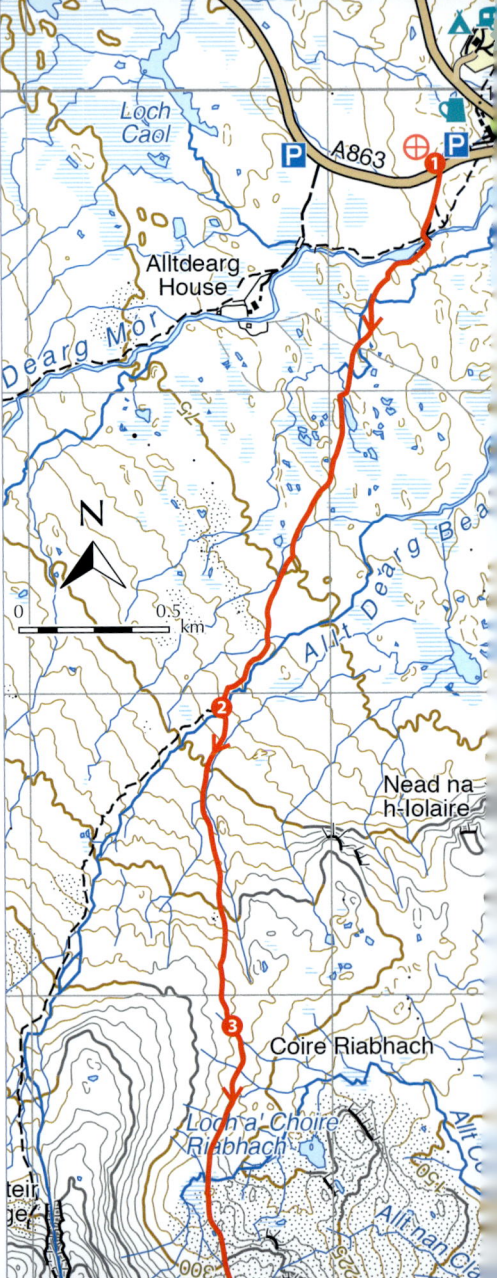

Route 1 – The Northern Three Munros

4 Do not cross the stream but ascend the bank to its right (north) side. Follow an ill-defined path up rocks and scree. Higher up, the path is more obvious and at about mid height, the scree slope twists to the right. Straight ahead is a steep crag with a distinctive arrow-like overhang. Turn left and ascend a steep, rocky gully which leads to a large cairn on the very lip of upper Coire Rhibach (NG 475 252).

5 From the cairn, the upper coire is a featureless place, a jumble of large boulders and scree. In poor visibility, it can be a difficult place to navigate.

Head up and left, picking your way over boulders to reach a scree path which zigzags up to a little col on the south-east ridge (NG 474 251) marked by a distinctive finger of rock above and left of it.

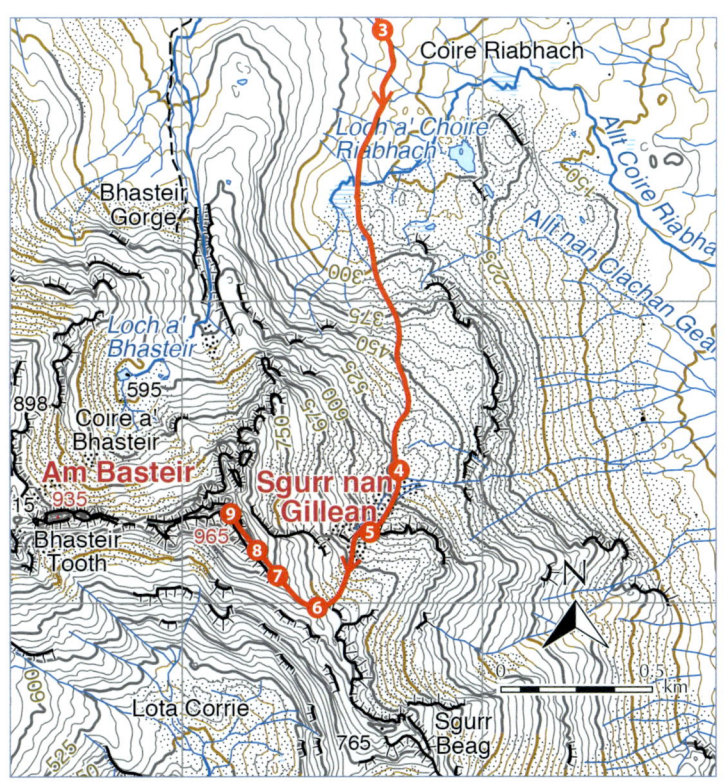

Approach to south-east ridge, Sgurr nan Gillean. The route from middle to upper coire.

South-east ridge. The route in the upper coire from the cairn and up to Sgurr nan Gillean

Skye Munros Topo Booklet

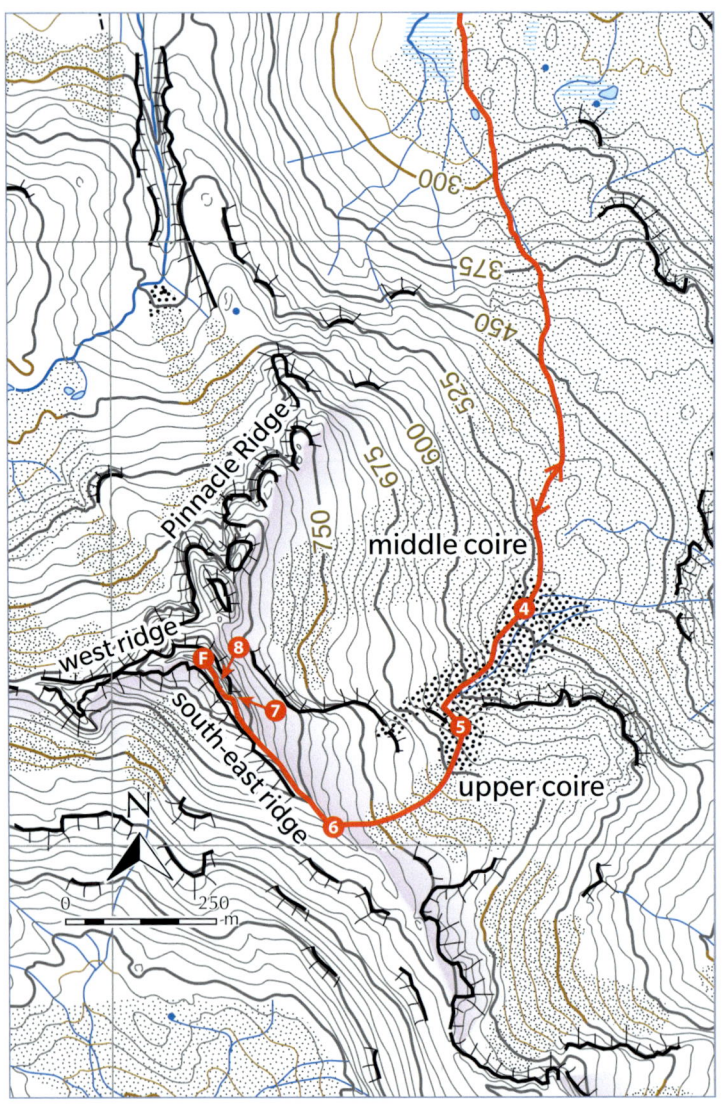

Route 1 – The Northern Three Munros

6 From the col, either scramble along the crest of the ridge or take a path to the right.

The ridge above can be taken by many lines. Generally, the more direct the line, the harder the terrain. Follow the ridge which eases you in gently, then keep to the left of the crest to avoid most difficulties.

7 At the first real steepening of the ridge the most obvious route is to head slightly left and go up a steep gully which has an awkward exit higher up. Head left to a distinctive basalt dyke higher up.

8 Ascend the dyke then head right towards the summit block which bars access to the top. Aim for a distinctive towering block on the skyline. A series of sloping ledges and corners rise from a smooth slab (which is slippery if wet). The climbing is easier than it looks from below. Climb the steps in the corner/rake. This is grade 2/3 but can feel more serious in poor conditions. There are good spike/block

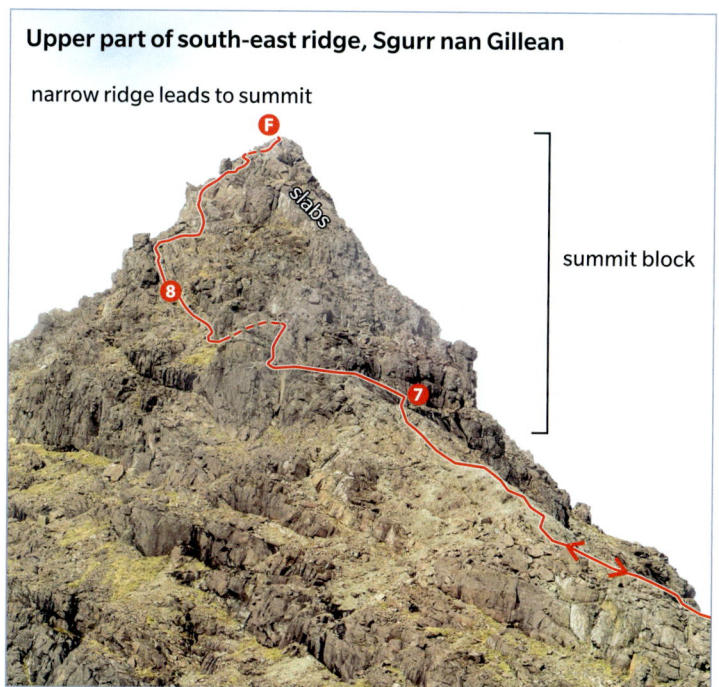

Upper part of south-east ridge, Sgurr nan Gillean

narrow ridge leads to summit

slabs

summit block

33

View from the south-east ridge showing the route across the upper coire to the base of the south-east ridge

belays above the awkward corner moves should a rope be needed.

Head right on easier terrain towards the crest of the ridge. Exit left from a small niche to emerge onto the ridge just above some cracked slabs.

Above the cracked slab, head right and up onto the final narrow, horizontal section which leads to the summit. There are big drops to either side and the exposure is huge, but the problem is more psychological than physical. The rock is grippy gabbro and the holds are good, so just focus on the task at hand rather than staring at the seemingly bottomless drops either side. This psychological crux crosses a narrow slab which has seen many people reduced to crawling. Don't be proud; just do what it takes. A final airy step across a narrow gap leads to the summit cairn of **Sgurr nan Gillean** and well-deserved views.

Descent: The easiest way is to retrace your route and descend the south-east ridge. The descent may seem more complex, especially the upper section. Return over the narrow

Route 1 – The Northern Three Munros

Summit and cairn on Sgurr nan Gillean

section for about 60m, then descend to the right to find the corner/rake you ascended. If you come to distinctive cracked slabs you have gone a few metres too far. Below the corner, follow the dyke line down to easier terrain, then locate the col and head for the cairn that marks the top of the gully leading down from upper Coire Rhibhach.

Route 2
The Central Two Munros

Sgurr a' Mhadaidh and Sgurr a' Ghreadaidh
And South Top of Sgurr a' Ghreadaidh and Sgurr Thormaid
And an option to include Sgurr na Banachdich

Start/finish	Park opposite Glen Brittle Youth Hostel (NG 409 225)
Time	6–7hr (for the two Munros)
Distance	9km
Total ascent/descent	1000m
Grade	Scrambling to grade 3
Warning	On typical guided courses this is likely to be a bad weather day option. If doing this route in inclement weather, take care and be aware of the conditions.

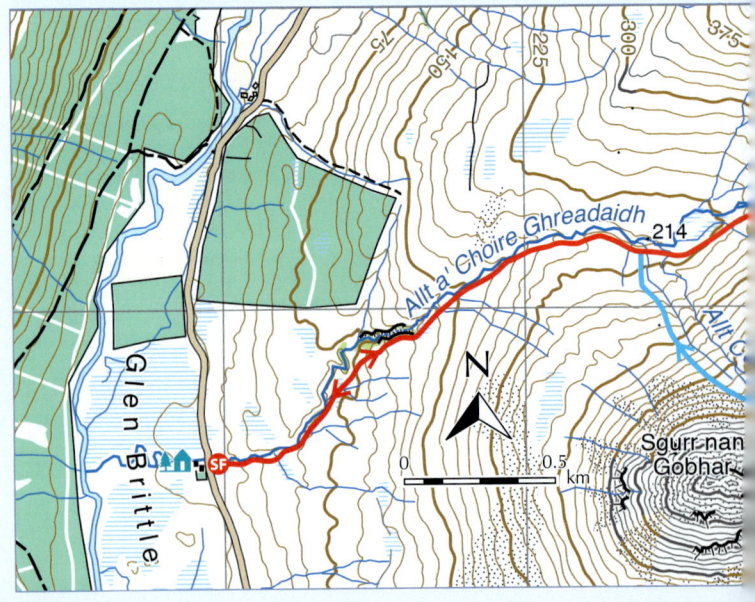

View north from the summit of Sgurr a Mhadaidh

These two Munros are included together because they are both accessed via the same walk in and are often climbed together. They are a good introduction to the next level of Cuillin Munros once you have tackled some of the easier walking ones. There is some scrambling but it's never too hard, exposed or sustained.

This route is often chosen for a bad weather option, the walk in being short and relatively easy and sheltered from strong south-westerly winds. It is a relatively easy way to bag two Munros which involve scrambling.

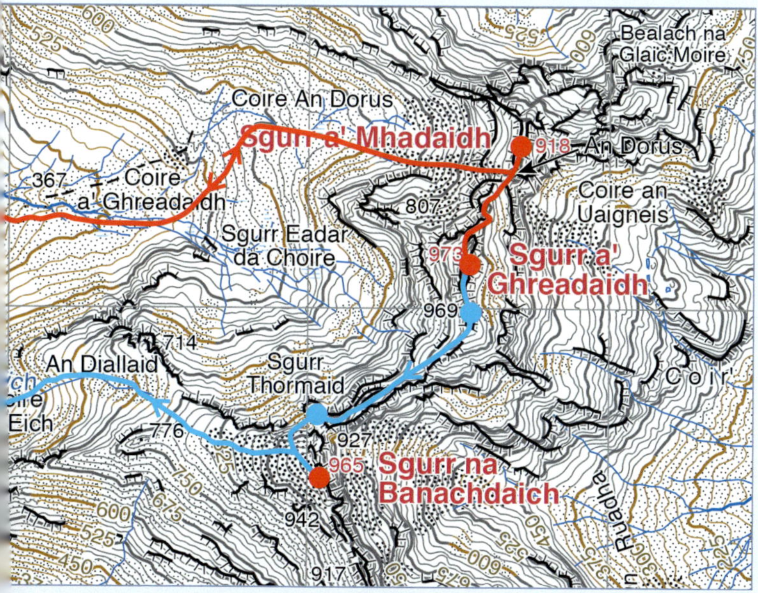

Approach to An Dorus

Start/finish	Park opposite Glen Brittle Youth Hostel (NG 409 225)
Time	1.5–2hr
Distance	4.4km
Total ascent/descent	830m
Grade	Mainly walking with a little grade 1 scrambling as you approach An Dorus
Warning	River/stream crossings can be problematic if in spate.

A walk mainly on a good path past beautiful waterfalls then a scree ascent with some easy scrambling to An Dorus.

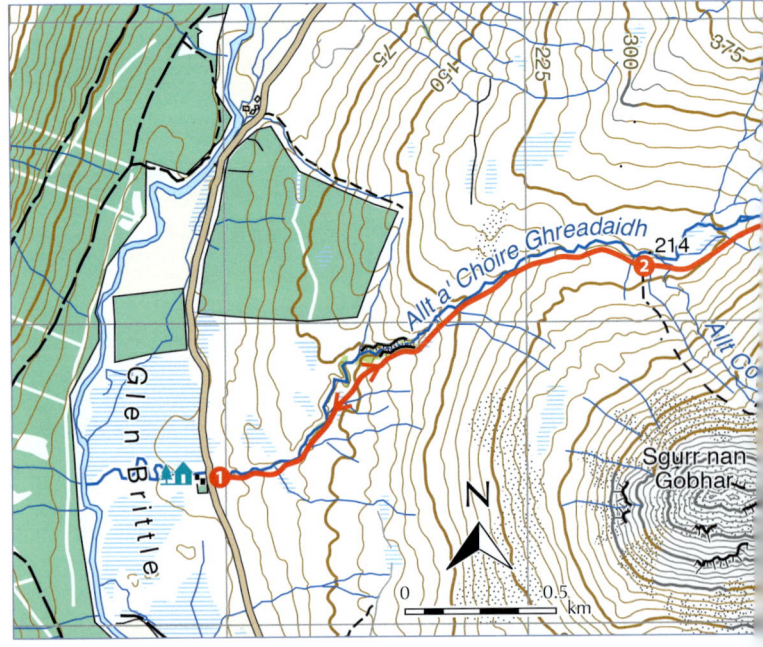

Route 2 – The Central Two Munros

❶ Park by Glen Brittle Youth Hostel and take the path which follows the **Allt a' Choire Ghreadaidh** upstream on its southern bank.

❷ Ignore turn offs to the right which are the route up Sgurr na Banachdich. Continue following the river upstream until you come to some slabs that form a lengthy water slide.

❸ At the top of the impressive water slide, head up right away from the river and follow traces of a path up into Coire a' Ghreadaidh. Steep terrain leads up to **Coire An Dorus**.

❹ Head right and up towards the screes visible below An Dorus. The terrain levels off.

❺ Before the ground rises to An Dorus, there is a good place to stop with a stream to fill water bottles and assorted boulders to lounge on (or shelter behind in bad weather!).

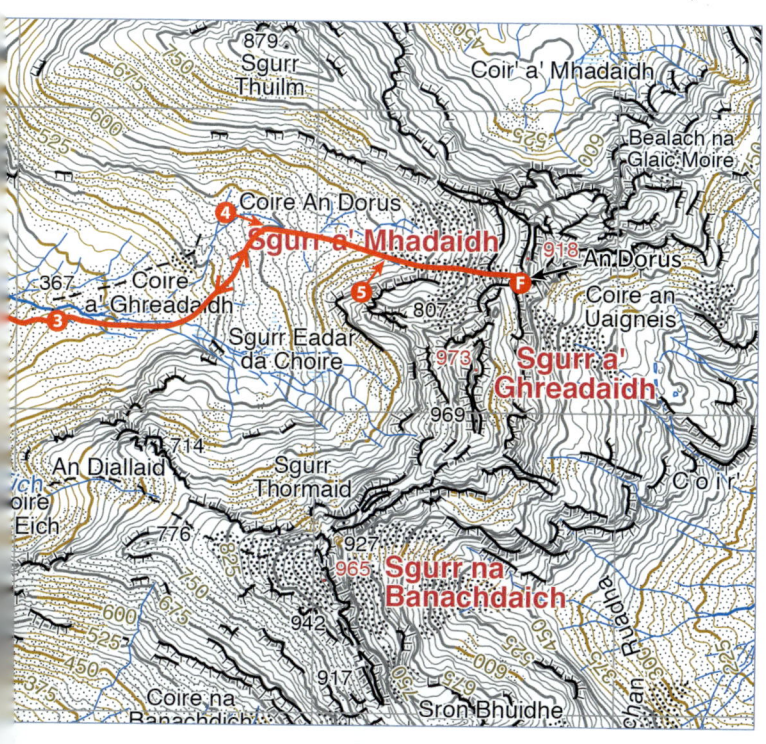

A path leads into a mini dry gorge then ascends scree and boulders, keeping tight in to the mini cliff to your right. Keep switched on and head out left and up then zigzag up the scree to An Dorus. In poor weather, this can be quite disorientating and people have been known to accidentally head up to Eag Dubh rather than An Dorus.

As the scree fan narrows, the way ahead becomes more defined by cliffs either side. If you have walking poles then consider leaving them here since you will want both hands for scrambling and you have to return this way (unless adding in the Munro Tops).

A section of easy hands-on scrambling leads to **An Dorus**. An Dorus, 'the door', certainly lives up to its name with a drop ahead down to the Coruisk basin and access to the two Munros left and right.

Sgurr a' Mhadaidh

Route	South-west ridge
Grade	Grade 2
Peak height	918m

This is the easier of the two so the best to go for first. It provides a good introduction to the Cuillin Munros that involve more than just walking. The scrambling difficulties are mainly confined to the exit from An Dorus, with only short, relatively easy steps that require hands-on scrambling afterwards.

❶ From An Dorus, ascend the left wall (to the north) which is quite steep but only for a few moves. Stand on an obvious block then move up and right before stepping back left. Above this, a gully can be ascended but be careful because of lots of loose rock. Better still, move left of the gully and ascend more solid rock.

❷ Follow a faint path, passing several stone bivi shelters then ascending up and right.

❸ Ascend an obvious fault line where scrambling up steps next to a chimney/crack leads to an intersection with the south-west ridge which comes in from the right. Easy scrambling leads to the summit of **Sgurr a' Mhadaidh**.

Descent: Retrace route to An Dorus.

Skye Munros Topo Booklet

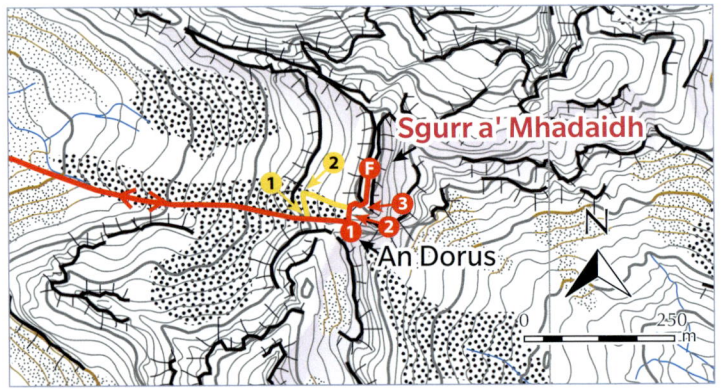

An Dorus to Sgurr a' Mhadaidh

Route 2 – The Central Two Munros

Bypass to avoid An Dorus

Note that the initial awkward exit from An Dorus can be bypassed by an easier alternative.

1 Instead of continuing up the scree to An Dorus, the bypass heads out left just before the final narrowing of the gully and the more scrambly section leading to An Dorus. This is about 40m below An Dorus. Head left on an indistinct path which slants up and left for about 60m.

2 Turn a corner right and then zigzag up rock and scree to pass several walled bivi sites and reach the main route to the summit. If you intend to descend the same way then take careful note of where you intersect the main route so you can find it on the way down.

A guide protects their client on the initial steep scramble to exit An Dorus and access Sgurr a' Mhadaidh

Sgurr a' Ghreadaidh

Route	North-north-east ridge
Grade	Grade 3
Peak height	973m

The crux is the exit from An Dorus, so keep in mind that you will have to reverse this on the descent. After the steep exit scramble the difficulties ease off, with stretches of walking and easy scrambling interspersed with short, harder scrambles.

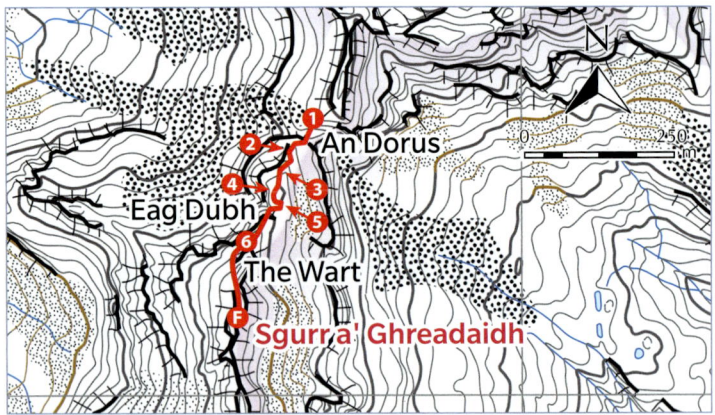

1 Climb out of An Dorus by a crack and corner to the right. This is steep grade 3 terrain but only for a few short moves.

There are anchors above the climber if a rope is used but satisfy yourself as to their integrity because the most obviously used block has cracks all around it.

Above the crux, the ground levels off and is followed at first on the Loch Coruisk side of the ridge before crossing to a path on the Glen Brittle side. Follow this path to a basalt dyke which cuts back up left.

2 Follow the dyke up to the crest of the ridge. Descend slightly on the Coruisk side and follow a path before heading up

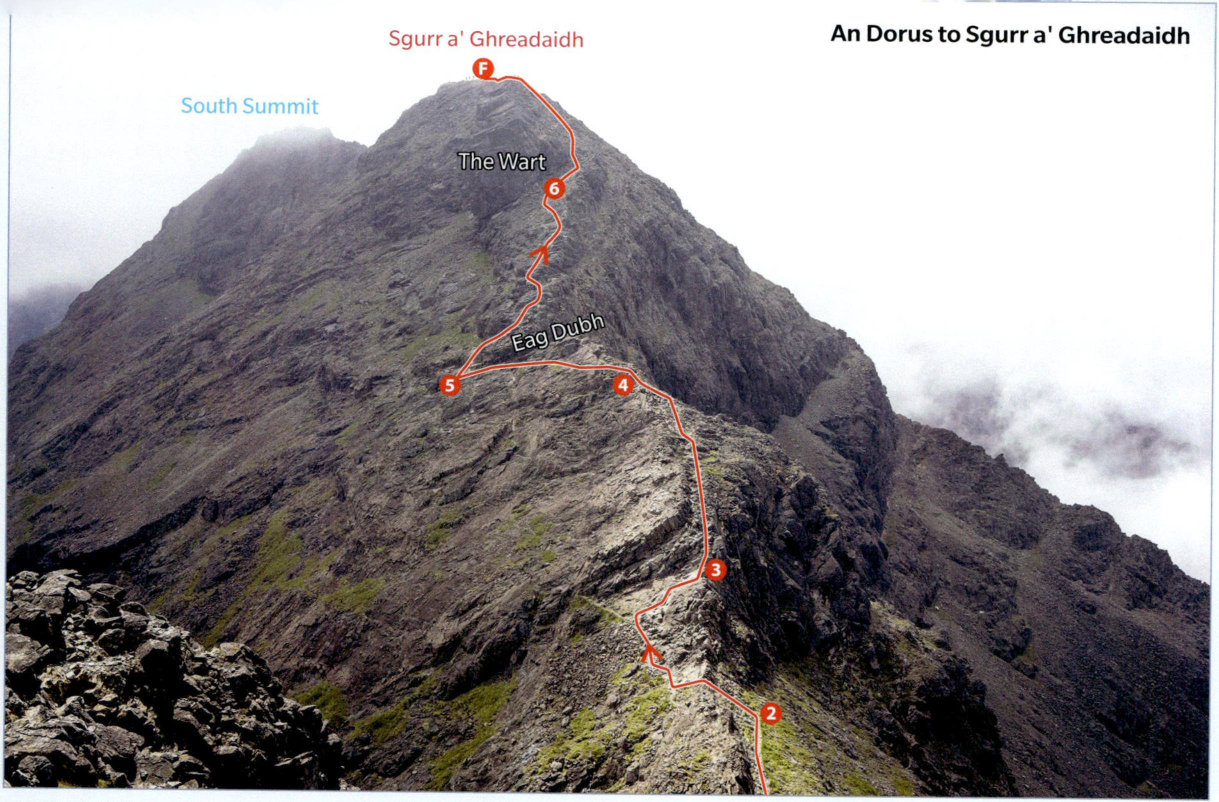
An Dorus to Sgurr a' Ghreadaidh
Sgurr a' Ghreadaidh
F
South Summit
The Wart
6
Eag Dubh
5
4
3
2

The climb out of (and back into) An Dorus is the crux of the route up Sgurr a' Ghreadaidh

slabs/corners to the right, ignoring the path which continues onwards.

❸ At the top of the slabs there are a steep couple of moves in an exposed position which lead to easier terrain. Continue easily, just slightly on the Glen Brittle side of the crest, then up to the crest of the ridge.

❹ Look for distinctive horizontal strata cutting left on the Coruisk side. Follow this to a path then descend slabs leftwards, parallel with the deep-cut chimney of **Eag Dubh**.

❺ Leave the base of Eag Dubh and head up slabs on the far side. Climb a steep overlap on good handholds (harder in descent) then head right up a corner before cutting back left and picking a line up to the base of the feature very aptly known as the **Wart**.

❻ The Wart looks impassable but is easily bypassed to the right. Scree and rock lead up past the Wart, and a short ascent takes you up onto a well-positioned horizontal ridge leading towards the summit.

Just before the summit, descend into a notch which bisects the ridge. Exit on the Glen Brittle side. A ledge leads up to the summit of **Sgurr a' Ghreadaidh** and a miniscule cairn. Further along the ridge is the South Summit (a Munro Top).

Descent: Return to An Dorus by the same route.

Route 2 – The Central Two Munros

Sgurr a' Ghreadaidh's South Top and Sgurr Thormaid (and Sgurr na Banachdich)

Route	South ridge of Sgurr a' Ghreadaidh, traverse of Sgurr Thormaid
Grade	Grade 3
Peak height	South Top 969m, Sgurr Thormaid 927m

Sgurr a' Ghreadaidh's South Summit is a good add-on to the main summit. Its south ridge can then be descended to take in the Munro Top of Sgurr Thormaid and the Munro Sgurr na Banachdich.

For a fit team, Sgurr a' Mhadaidh and Sgurr a' Ghreadaidh make for a relatively short day, so it makes sense to add on these Tops. The narrow arête leading to the South Top gets a lot of hype, being, according to www.walkhighlands.co.uk, 'the narrowest arête in the British Isles – sharp as a razor'. This may be a bit of an exaggeration and the difficulties are perhaps more psychological than physical. The scrambling is probably no harder than the climb out of An Dorus but it is sustained, and the route is committing since there is no feasible escape route before Sgurr na Banachdich. It is a route for the experienced and hill-fit scrambler.

A The South Top is only about 170m from the main summit but the terrain is complex and challenging. The ridge can be taken direct but the route below is easier and avoids an awkward descent of a nose.

Follow the ridge towards the South Top for a few metres then, as it widens out, descend on the Glen Brittle side for a few metres. Turn left and descend an awkward corner to reach ledges which contour round to the left.

Negotiate the next part of the ridge to the right then drop down to the start of the exposed arête which leads to the South Top.

B Cross a slab then traverse the narrow arête with an exposed and awkward step down at one point. Easier terrain then leads to the **South Top**.

C The best way to continue is to descend the south ridge directly, with much variation possible. This is exposed to start with but as height is lost, it becomes easier and less of a knife edge.

It is possible to bypass many of the difficulties by retracing your route until just before the arête and descending a gully on the Glen Brittle side. This is a mix of scree and loose rocks on slabs,

Skye Munros Topo Booklet

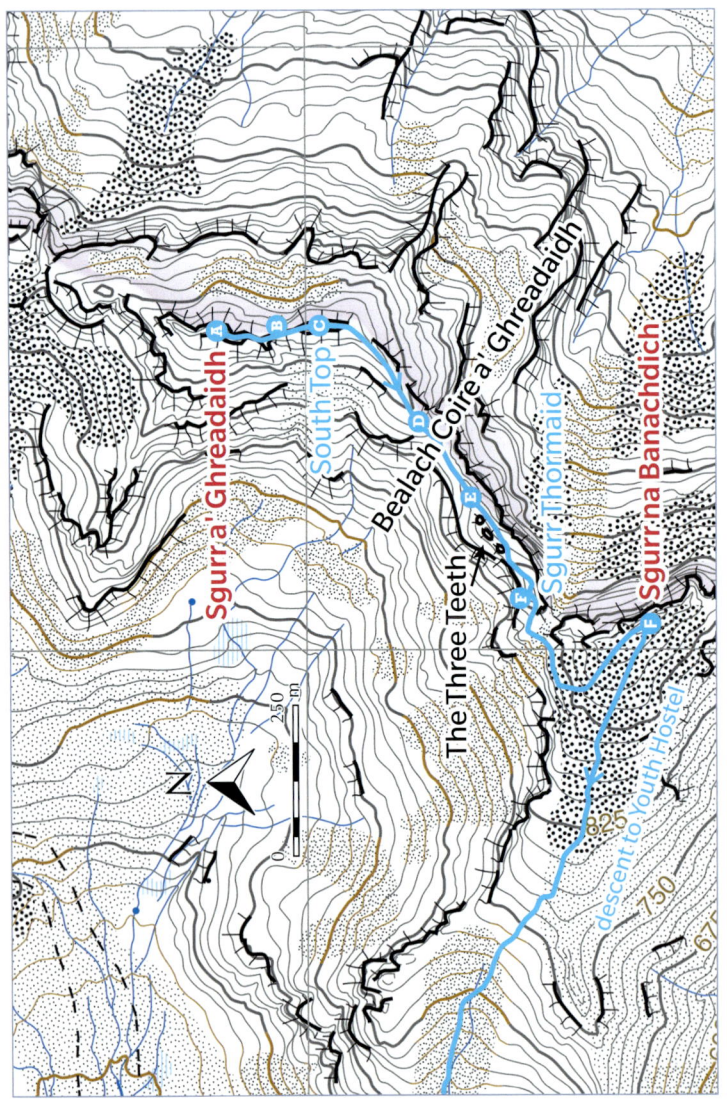

Sgurr a' Ghreadaidh to Sgurr Thormaid and Sgurr na Banachdich

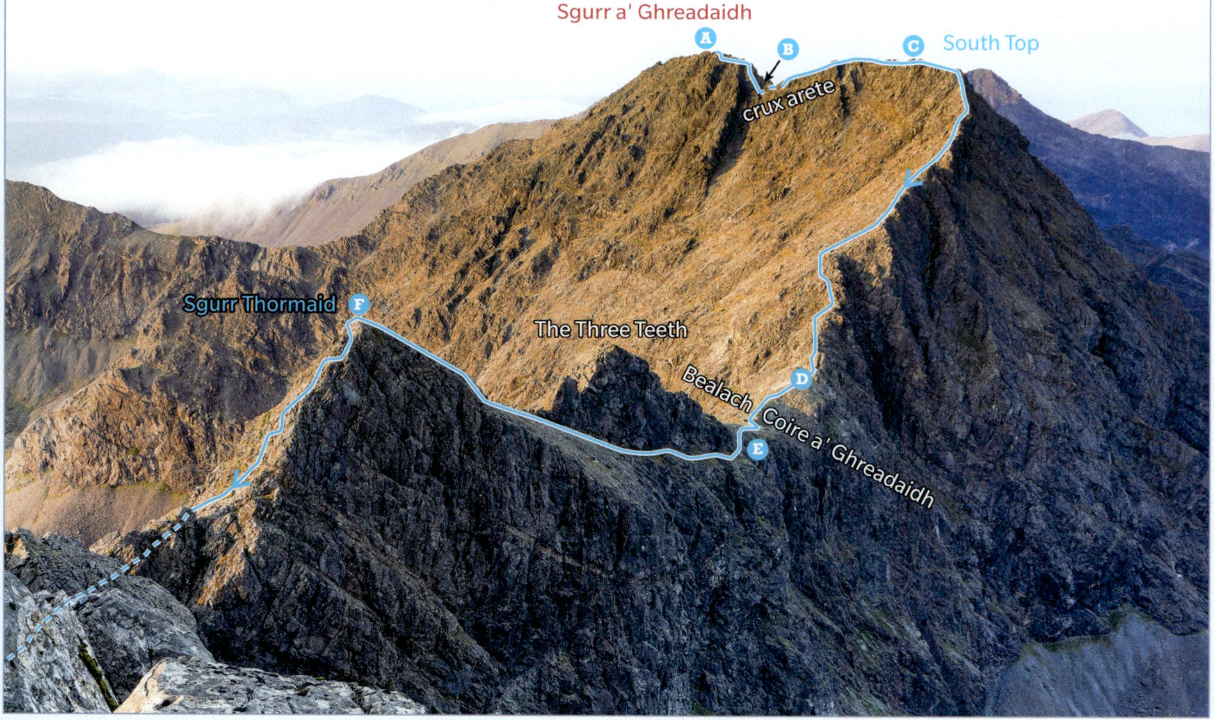
Sgurr a' Ghreadaidh
A
B
C
South Top
crux arete
Sgurr Thormaid
F
The Three Teeth
D
Bealach
Coire a' Ghreadaidh
E

Guided group on the crux arête as they head to the South Top of Sgurr a' Ghreadaidh

and leads down to a traverse line which contours across to rejoin the south ridge below the difficulties.

D **Bealach Coire a' Ghreadaidh** is the low point at the base of the south ridge with several stone bivi circles.

E Ahead are the **Three Teeth** which are best bypassed on the left. Descend slightly then contour around below the Teeth to reach slabs leading up to **Sgurr Thormaid**.

F From Sgurr Thormaid, the descent is tricky and the best line not obvious from above. Be very careful since there are huge drops to the left.

From the summit, head towards Sgurr na Banachdich and descend a short groove, then turn right and work your way down a groove then a chimney to reach easier terrain. Scree and rock steps lead down to Bealach Thormaid.

The ascent to Sgurr na Banachdich can be confusing, especially in poor visibility. Exit the bealach and work your way up scree and rotten rocks, heading up and then rightwards to emerge on the west flank. Head up to the summit of **Sgurr na Banachdich**.

Do not try to go too directly from the bealach to the summit of Sgurr na Banachdich because of steep cliffs and big drops.

Descent: Descend the west flank into Coire an Eich and return to YHA. See Route 2 overview map.

Route 3
The South Central Three Munros

Sgurr Mhic Choinnich, the Inaccessible Pinnacle, and Sgurr na Banachdich
And Sgurr na Banachdich's South Top and Sgurr Thormaid

Start/finish	Car park at end of road immediately before Glen Brittle Campsite (NG 409 206)
Time	8–9hr
Distance	12km
Total ascent/descent	1400m
Grade	Sustained scrambling, climbing to Moderate and an abseil
Warning	A mentally and physically challenging day, especially for non-climbers. The Inaccessible Pinnacle is the only Munro you may have to queue up for, especially if the forecast is good.

For many, this will be the day they have been dreading. The Inaccessible Pinnacle has a fearsome reputation and most people will find this a psychologically tough day. It involves sustained scrambling on Sgurr Mhic Choinnich, exposed climbing and an abseil off the In Pinn, then a less demanding walk across to Sgurr na Banachdich.

The Inaccessible Pinnacle above a sea of clouds with Sgurr nan Gillean to the left and Bla Bheinn to the right

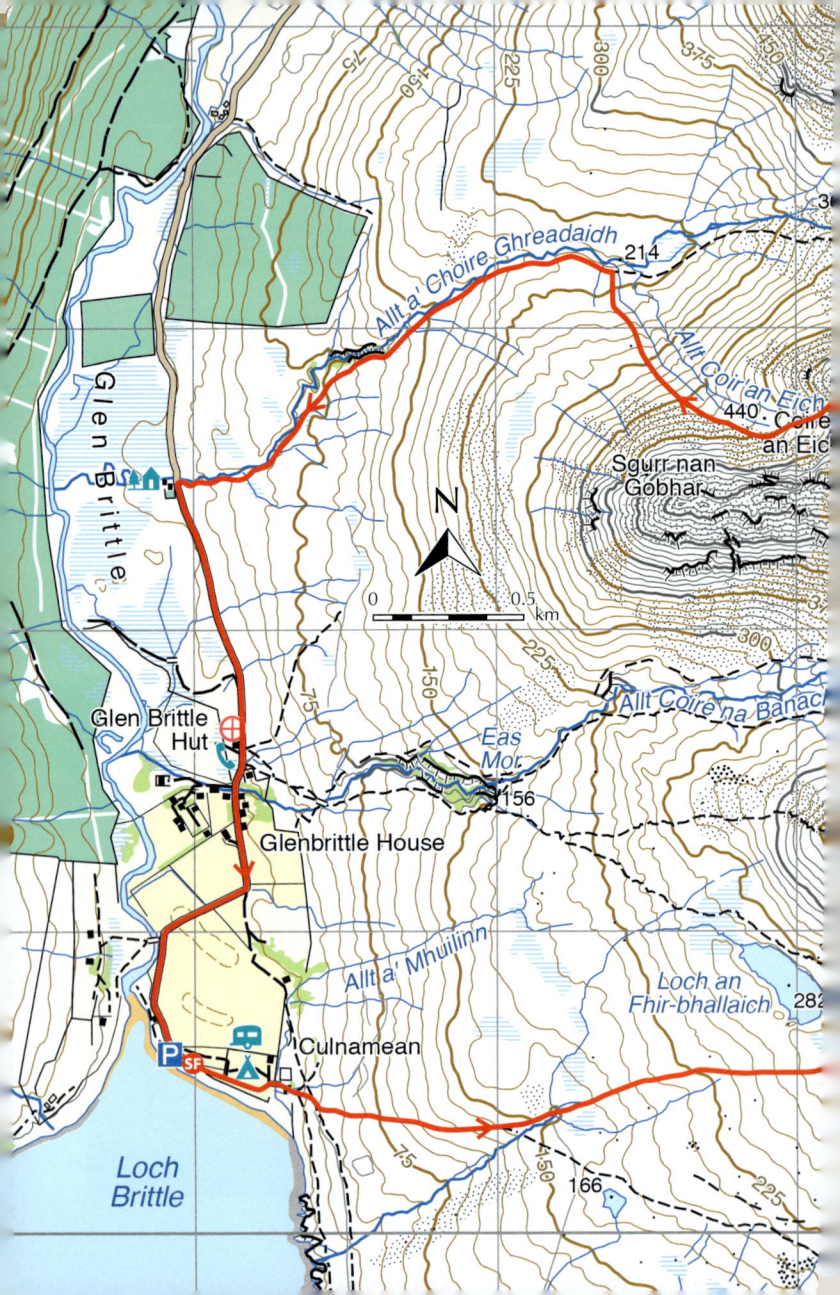

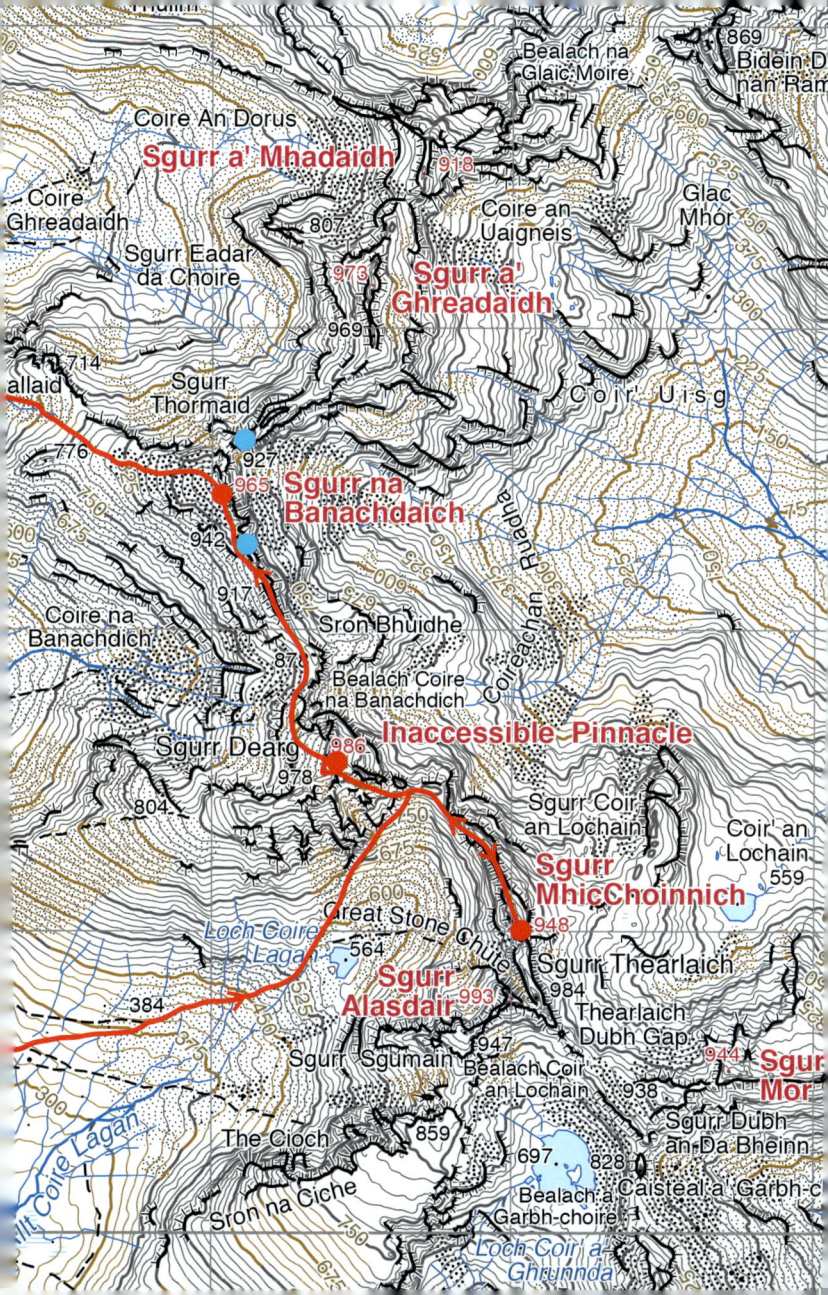

Skye Munros Topo Booklet

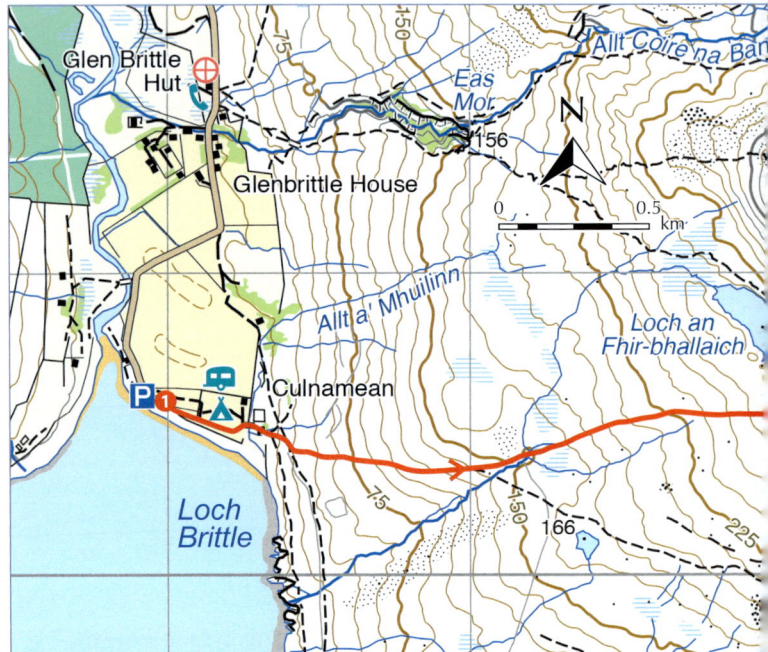

Approach to Coire Lagan

Start/finish	Car park at end of road immediately before Glen Brittle Campsite (NG 409 206)
Time	1–1.25hr
Distance	3.6km
Total ascent/descent	535m
Grade	Mainly a walk on a path, with an easy gully scramble just below the coire.

This is a beautiful walk in its own right and offers great views and interesting geological features such as the glaciated slabs at the entrance to the coire.

Route 3 – The South Central Three Munros

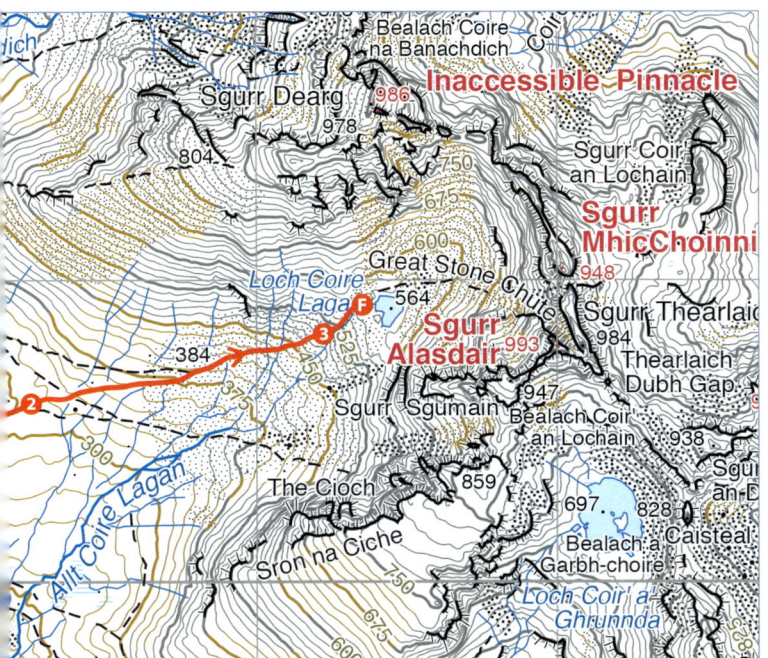

1 Park immediately before Glen Brittle Campsite. If this is full then you can pay to park on the campsite itself. The campsite shop does fantastic coffee and croissants.

Walk through the campsite and exit via the path left of the shower block. Ascend to a major path above. Turn right on this, then almost immediately left to follow the path that leads to Coire Lagan. Ignore a turning on the right which leads to Coir' a' Ghrunnda.

2 Ignore a path coming in from the left by a huge cairn and continue to reach a short cliff, seemingly barring further progress.

3 An easy scramble up a gully between slabs leads to a path that zigzags up next to the exit stream from **Loch Coire Lagan**.

Sgurr Mhic Choinnich

Route	An Stac Screes, then the north-west ridge
Grade	Grade 2 Scramble
Peak height	948m

Sgurr Mhic Choinnich is one of the harder Cuillin Munros. Do not be fooled by the low grade. The scrambling is sustained, if not overly hard. A tough scree approach followed by an exposed ridge with drops either side makes this a challenging route. The upper ridge consists of basalt slabs which can be treacherous in the wet.

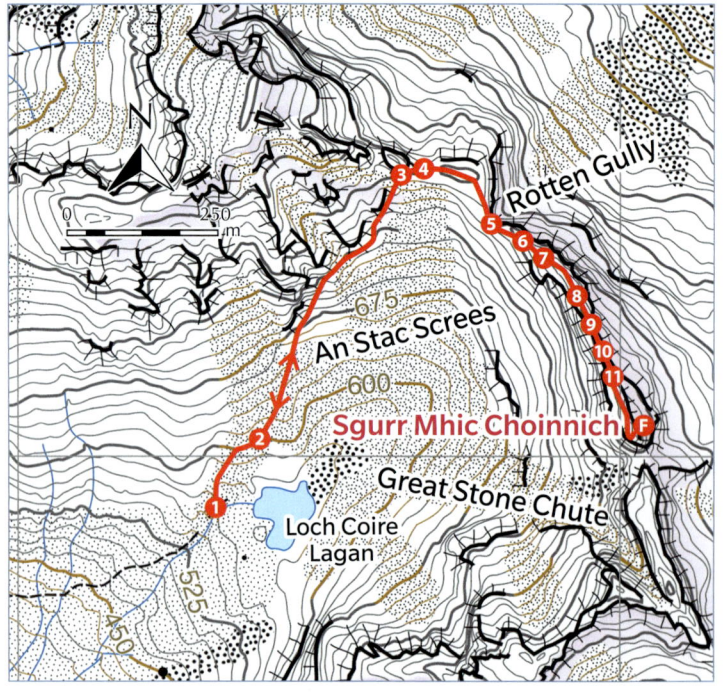

Slabs high on Sgurr Mhic Choinnich with In Pinn, Sgurr na Banachdich, Sgurr a' Ghreadaidh and Sgurr a' Mhadaidh in the distance

❶ Traditionally people take the An Stac Screes direct, but there is a much easier way which is much kinder to the environment than dislodging yet more scree. This takes more of a rising line, contouring around to meet the scree.

As you approach the coire, slabby rock faces to your left are inscribed with graffiti. Bear left and follow a rudimentary path which crosses boulders and scree in a rising diagonal above the loch.

❷ Reach a mini stone shelter and cairn. Leave the boulders to traverse scree then continue up and follow a line where the main An Stac Screes intersect with the rock above.

Continue up the scree until you reach a small cave tucked in on your left.

❸ Take note of the cave since it marks the start of the An Stac Bypass which leads up to the Inaccessible Pinnacle. It also makes a good place to potentially cache packs before going out and back to Sgurr Mhic Choinnich. Continue up and right of the cave then head up to the crest of the ridge above. Carry on along the ridge until a fin of rock bars your way.

❹ Turn left towards the Loch Coruisk side of the ridge. Scramble around the end of the fin to reach a level path which leads up onto a plateau which is crossed. Descend to the head of **Rotten Gully**.

❺ Continue towards Sgurr Mhic Choinnich, ascending scree and rocky

The initial steep scrambling, Sgurr Mhic Choinich

terrain to a levelling off before the start of the scrambling proper.

❻ Steep ground bars the way ahead and the challenge looks formidable but, as long as the easiest line is taken, the scrambling is just a series of steps up short boulder-type problems.

As you approach the steep wall ahead, turn left for a few metres then ascend steeply up ledges and follow a crack rightwards below a distinct

Route 3 – The South Central Three Munros

light-coloured rock. Continue right then back left to ascend a gully at the top of which an awkward scramble leads to a jumble of boulders. Traverse right on easier ground.

Cut back left and ascend steeply.

7 Turn right to cross distinctive cracked slabs then continue a rising traverse up easier terrain, still on the Coire Lagan side of the ridge. The route now starts to become exposed as you descend into a distinct notch which bisects the ridge.

8 Exit the notch, then either climb the short but steep wall ahead or traverse it in an exposed position to the right. Continue along a faint path then ascend to another notch in the ridge. At the time of writing, this gully is jammed with precariously balanced boulders which present a real danger. Try to avoid them to the left then traverse above them.

9 Exit the notch via a slab and gain the ridge line where the going is easy. A horizontal path leads towards the summit.

10 Descend slightly to the left of the crest then ascend to rock steps and slabs leading up to a ledge. The right end of the ledge descends via a chimney and leads to the start of **Collie's Ledge**.

11 The left end of the ledge is blocked by a steep cliff and the route heads out around an overhang to the left. A few moves of exposed scrambling leads to a narrow ledge. Scramble across a gap in the ledge and continue in the same line across a series of ledges and short steps, weaving a line across the upper basalt slabs. These slabs can be very slippery if wet and there are huge drops off to the left.

Continue along a ledge/path until a short steep wall blocks progress. Scramble up a series of steps then continue in the same direction until another short wall bars the way. Another short scramble arcs up and right to reach slabs just below the summit block.

Head up the slabs. You will now be in an exposed position with drops down into Coire Lagan. Turn left and follow ledges below the summit block, then scramble up and back left to reach the broken memorial stone and summit cairn of **Sgurr Mhic Choinnich**.

Descent: By the same route. Return to the small cave at the top of An Stac Screes.

Linking Sgurr Mhic Choinnich and the Inaccessible Pinnacle

Route	South-east flank of Sgurr Dearg or An Stac Bypass
Grade	Grade 1–2

This is a relatively easy link up but the terrain is loose with lots of scree and evidence of rockfall. There is also a risk of rocks being dislodged from above by people accessing the Inaccessible Pinnacle.

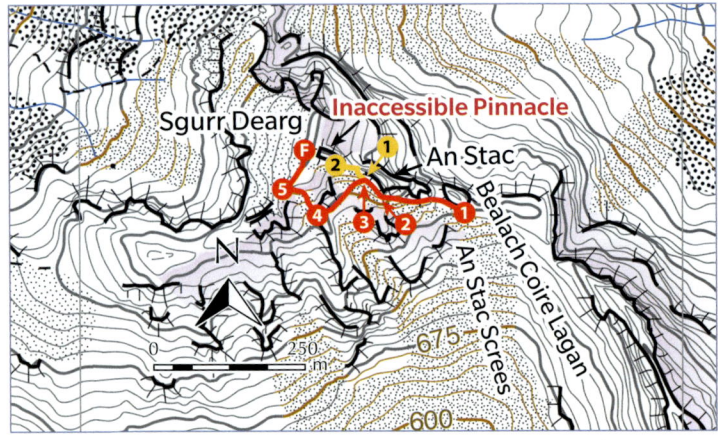

❶ From the cave at the top of the An Stac Screes, go up a scree path then an orange slab which skirts beneath the imposing bulk of An Stac.

❷ Pass behind some large boulders and turn right and follow distinct strata rightwards just above scree. (**①** Traditionally, the route continues by scrambling up to a higher, parallel ramp line, a brown slab which is ascended direct to the Inaccessible Pinnacle **②** This brown slab is particularly exposed to any rockfall dislodged from above by people descending to the In Pinn.)

❸ For a safer route, do not scramble up to the higher ramp line but instead turn left and take a scree path which contours around below a cave.

Skye Munros Topo Booklet

View of climbers accessing the Inaccessible Pinnacle by the An Stac bypass. Sgurr Alasdair and Great Stone Chute in background

④ Beyond the cave, zigzag up scree and blocks to reach Sgurr Dearg's west ridge.

⑤ Follow the west ridge upwards, initially on a horizontal ledge on the Coire Banachdich side. Head up to the crest of the ridge and continue to the summit of **Sgurr Dearg**, a large flat area overlooking the In Pinn.

The Inaccessible Pinnacle

Route	East ridge, 65m
Grade	Moderate with an abseil descent of the west ridge
Peak height	986m

The steep, vertical west ridge faces Sgurr Dearg and will be the line of descent by abseil. Most people will climb the gentler angled east ridge, a relatively easy rock climb with mostly large footholds and handholds.

Route 3 – The South Central Three Munros

While not too physically difficult, the route is very exposed with huge drops either side. The main problem is often psychological. In anything other than ideal conditions, the In Pinn will feel much harder. It can be exposed to the wind, and can feel tricky if the rock is wet.

❶ From a distinct notch, head down the slabs which lead to the base of the In Pinn. Descend straight down then head right before zigzagging down then heading back left to the base of the Pinn.

❷ Below the In Pinn is a large platform with plenty of space, but be aware of any climbers above who may dislodge rocks.

The Inaccessible Pinnacle

The Inaccessible Pinnacle

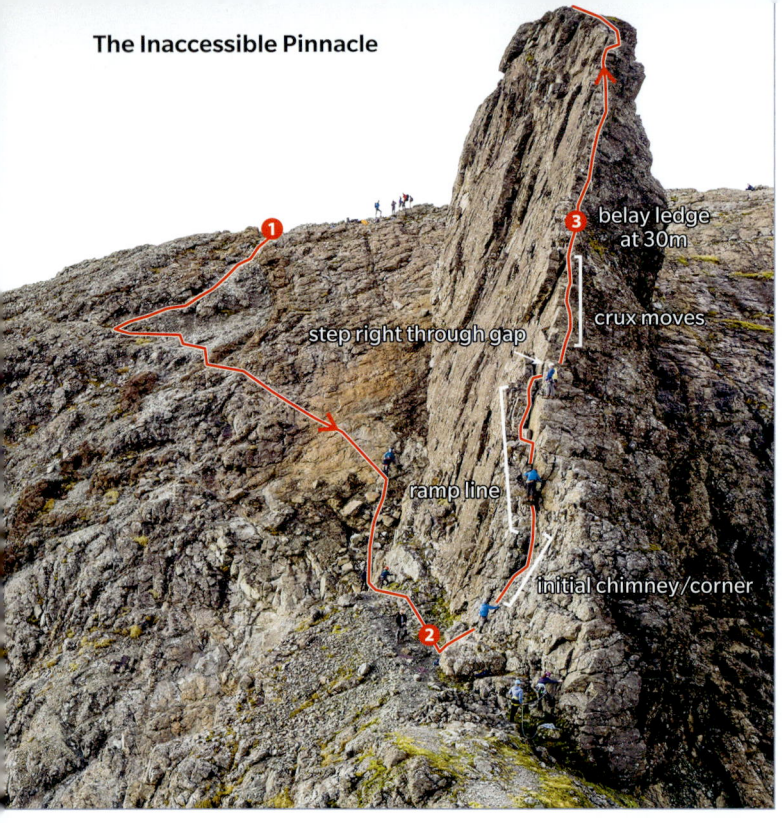

The climb starts approximately 8m before the lowest point of the east ridge.

Climb up a broken chimney, then ascend up and left along a ramp line which is parallel to the actual crest of the ridge and a bit lower.

Gain the crest of the ridge by stepping right through a notch. Whereas before there was only exposure to your left, now there is also a massive drop to your right. Above are the hardest moves on the whole route, the crux. A flake/spike can be used to protect the crux moves which lead to the belay ledge.

The crux is only short but the handholds may not be as good as hoped for and for a move or two, the footholds are decidedly lacking. On the plus side, the belay is just above. Your leader will be securely anchored and can give you a tight rope, both to add psychological security but also as a physical aid.

The belay is at about 30m and is a small ledge. A large block can be used as an anchor.

How it feels to have bagged the In Pinn

❸ The second pitch of 35m is easier, but do not get overconfident since the ridge is still very exposed and not a place to fall.

Towards the top, the ridge widens. Large blocks serve as belay anchors.

❹ The summit. The belay is just before smooth ledges which lead around the base of the **Bolster Stone** (the highest point on the In Pinn) to the metal anchors for the abseil.

Most will be happy to have made it this far but some will want to touch or even stand on the Bolster Stone. It is not too hard to ascend, but remember you will have to down climb it. The rope will be below you for this, so if you were to fall you would hit the ledges below.

A metal strap around the base of the Bolster Stone provides the anchors for the abseil to regain terra firma. It's only a short abseil (less than 20m) but can appear quite daunting.

From the base of the abseil, walk carefully back up the slabs to where you left your packs on Sgurr Dearg.

Route 3 – The South Central Three Munros

Sgurr Dearg to Sgurr na Banachdich

Route	South ridge
Grade	Grade 1 (but grade 2 if South Top taken in)
Peak height	965m

This is an easy ridge traverse with fantastic views and can feel like a reward after the intensity of the In Pinn.

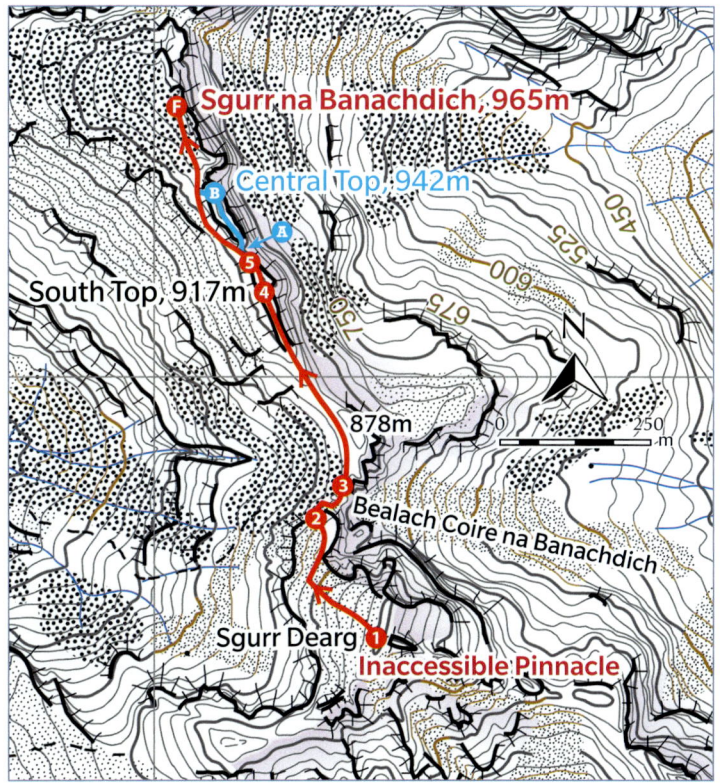

Route 3 – The South Central Three Munros

❶ Descend Sgurr Dearg's north-west flank (a grade 1 scramble). Zigzag down the screes, taking care to stay well clear of the steep cliffs to the east.

❷ The descent into **Bealach Coire na Banachdich** is a short scramble and can be slippery in the wet. Exit the bealach, descending slightly on the Glen Brittle side then contouring around to the right.

❸ A path of sorts leads up and across scree, bypassing **Point 878m** to reach the south ridge proper.

Sgurr na Banachdich via the south ridge

Most of the difficulties can be bypassed by taking an easier line on the Glen Brittle side, but the direct line of the crest itself offers more challenging scrambling.

Easy scrambling leads to the **South Top**.

❹ Beyond the narrow South Top, many will opt for the easiest line which descends a bit on the Glen Brittle side before narrow ledges contour round below the Central Top to reach a small col.

Ⓐ Some will want to bag the Central Top as it is a Munro Top. This is steeper and a grade 2 scramble. Take the easiest line on the crest of the ridge.

Ⓑ Reach the **Central Top** of Sgurr na Banachdich. After traversing the top, scramble down steeply on the western side to reach a small col and rejoin the main route.

Heading up the south ridge of Sgurr na Banachdich with the Central Top in the background

5 From the col, scramble up a series of rocky steps to reach a horizontal ledge leading north to the summit of **Sgurr na Banachdich**.

Descent: The route back to the Youth Hostel is just rough walking but some may wish to bag another Munro Top first.

Sgurr Thormaid

Route	South-west ridge
Grade	Grade 2
Peak height	927m

At the end of a long day, the route to Sgurr Thormaid might take an hour out and back since it involves a lot of height loss and gain.

For map see Descent from Sgurr na Banachdich.

1 Descend from the summit in a north-westerly direction.

A Descend scree and rocks to the bealach between Sgurr na Banachdich and Sgurr Thormaid. Scramble up rocks beyond the bealach, with ever bigger drops down onto the scree below the bealach. This is serious scrambling with the potential to fall a long way and has been the site of an accident, so take care. Head leftwards, then back right and up a steep gully which leads up to slabs and the summit of **Sgurr Thormaid**.

Retrace your route and join the descent route from Sgurr na Banachdich.

Descent from Sgurr na Banachdich

Route	Western flank down into Coire an Eich
Grade	Rough walking

The descent is straightforward but in poor visibility the terrain can be confusing, so take care.

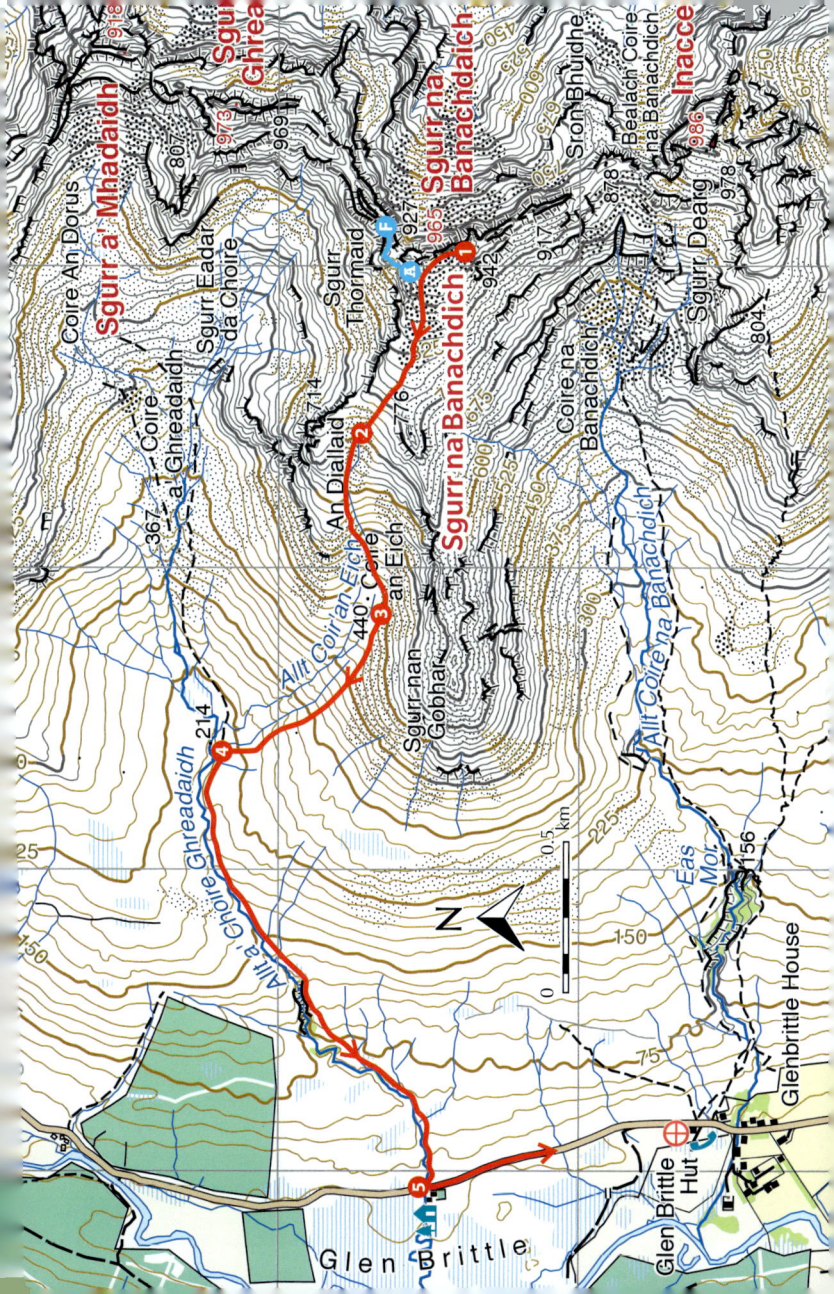

Route 3 – The South Central Three Munros

1 From the summit, descend traces of path over scree then cut down right to reach the ridge which leads out to An Diallaid.

2 Descend into **Coire an Erich** following a fairly distinct trail over scree.

3 Once off the screes, the going suddenly becomes much easier. Signs of a path lead down to the major path which heads up to An Dorus.

4 Turn left on the major path and go past delightful waterfalls to reach the road.

5 From the **Youth Hostel**, turn left on the road and follow it 2.5km back to the campsite.

Sgurr Dearg/The Inaccessible Pinnacle via Sgurr Dearg's west ridge

Start/finish	Car parking opposite Glen Brittle Memorial Hut (NG 412 216)
Time	5–7hr
Distance	7km
Total ascent/descent	975m
Grade	Sustained scrambling, climbing to Moderate and an abseil
Warning	A mentally and physically challenging day, especially for non-climbers. The Inaccessible Pinnacle is the only Munro you may have to queue up for, especially if the forecast is good.

This route is included as a means of climbing just the In Pinn. It will probably be the route taken by guided parties just doing the In Pinn.

1 Park opposite the Glen Brittle Memorial Hut then walk south along the road for about 50m to where a path by sheep pens heads towards the Cuillin.

Follow the path, cross the river by a bridge and continue up past the waterfall, Eas Mor.

2 At the path junction above the waterfall, take the path round to the right.

3 Take a turning on the left after about 250m. This is a smaller path and in poor conditions it is possible to miss it.

Skye Munros Topo Booklet

Heading up the west ridge of Sgurr Dearg

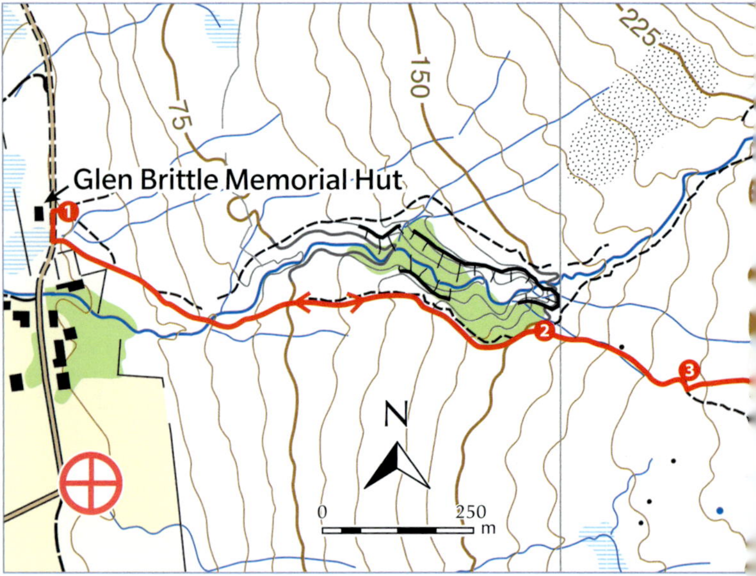

Glen Brittle Memorial Hut

Route 3 – The South Central Three Munros

The path heads up the west ridge, going over open moorland, gradually ascending.

Zigzag up scree and head for a crag with a distinct basalt chimney.

❹ Scramble up the chimney (a good warm up for things to come) or contour round and up further to the left. A good path now leads onwards and upwards.

Above the terrain levels off, then starts to rise once again with the way zigzagging up scree and boulders.

❺ At another levelling off just below Pt. 929 m (known as Sgurr Dearg Beag), head to the left then up scree, then head back up and right towards a distinctive notch. Scramble up to the left of the notch.

Once above the notch, contour around a bit below the summit of **Sgurr Dearg Beag** to reach an obvious col before the upper part of the west ridge.

❻ Above the col, the ridge becomes much narrower and more defined. The easiest line is a path just right of the crest which leads to a series of narrow ledges. These are not difficult but are very exposed, with a big drop on the right down into Coire Lagan.

The ledges lead to a path which comes to an end below a short gully leading up left.

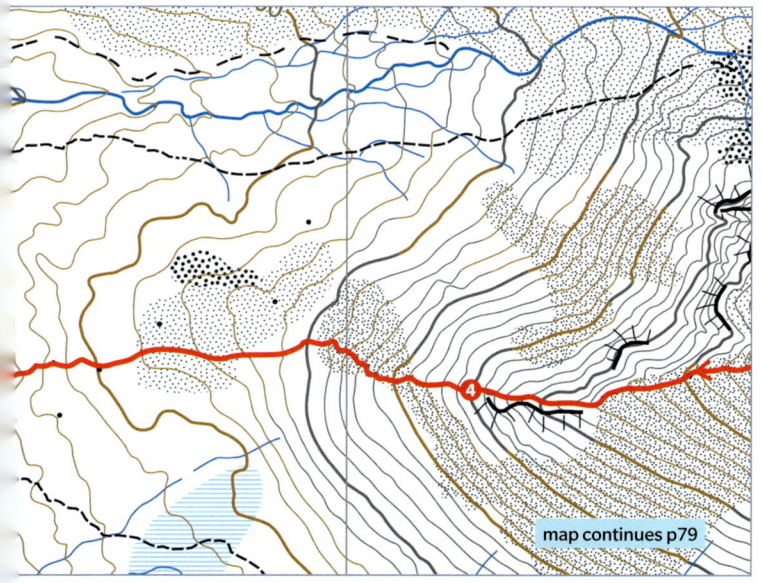

map continues p79

Route 3 – The South Central Three Munros

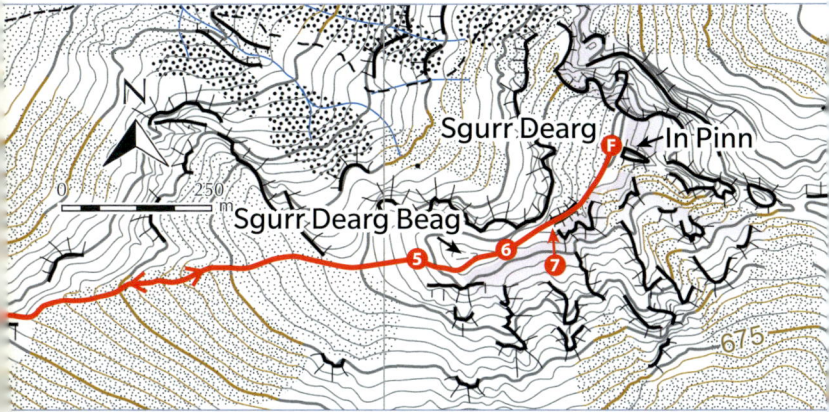

7 Scramble up the gully and exit it on the right then follow the ridge, staying a bit below the crest on the Coire Lagan side.

Almost at the top of the ridge, a short, steeper section is bypassed by ledges to the left of the crest. These lead up to the summit of **Sgurr Dearg**.

For description on climbing the In Pinn, see Inaccessible Pinnacle.

Descent: Quickest and easiest is to descend the ascent route.

Route 4
The Southern Three Munros

Sgurr nan Eag, Sgurr Dubh Mor and Sgurr Alasdair
And Munro Tops of Sgurr Dubh an Da Bheinn,
Sgurr Sgumain and Sgurr Thearlaich

Start/finish	NG 409 206 Glen Brittle beach car park by entrance to campsite. Additional parking available on campsite
Time	9–11hr
Distance	12.5km
Total ascent/descent	1450m
Grade	Scrambling to grade 3
Warning	A physically demanding day. Navigation to Sgurr Dubh Mor can be problematic in poor visibility.

Sgurr Dubh Mor and Sgurr Dubh an Da Bheinn seen from Sgurr Sgumain

The southern three Munros are often done as one fairly long day but can easily be split into two or three trips depending on your fitness levels, experience and confidence. All three share the same walk in to Coir' a' Ghrunnda.

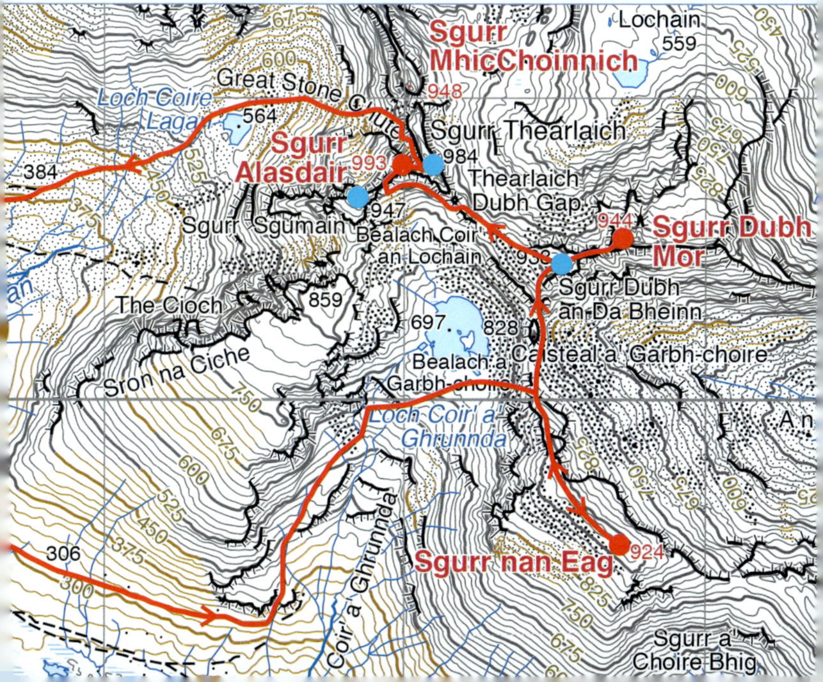

Approach to Coir' a' Ghrunnda

Start/finish	NG 409 206 Glen Brittle beach car park
Time	1.5–2hr
Distance	5.5km
Total ascent/descent	585m
Grade	Mainly walking with a little grade 1 scrambling
Warning	The two streams after the initial turning right to leave the Coire Lagan path can be impassable in spate.

A delightful walk mainly on a good path, then easy scrambling through amazing rock architecture leads to Coir a Ghrunnda.

Route 4 – The Southern Three Munros

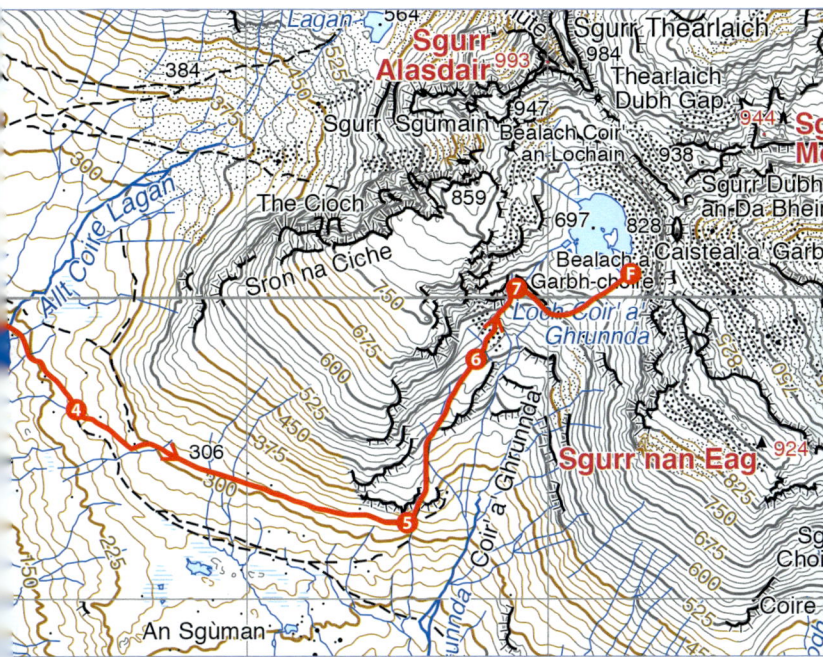

① Walk through the campsite and head up the path to the left of the shower block. Join a track, and turn right then almost immediately left to take the path up towards Coire Lagan.

② Take a fork right (NG 420 203) and cross a stream. If water levels are high then this crossing may be dangerous or impossible. Take note because the next stream crossing is wider.

③ Cross another stream (**Allt Coire Lagan**). After almost 400m there is a path junction.

④ At the path junction (NG 434 196), take the left turn and follow the path up past an obvious perched boulder on the left.

⑤ The path bears left steeply towards Coir' a' Ghrunnda via a rocky gully. Above, the path zigzags up scree. Higher up, the route becomes less distinct and the way up to Loch Coir' a' Ghrunnda is not that obvious, especially in poor visibility.

⑥ At NG 447 198, the path splits and there's a choice of either going through

Route 4 – The Southern Three Munros

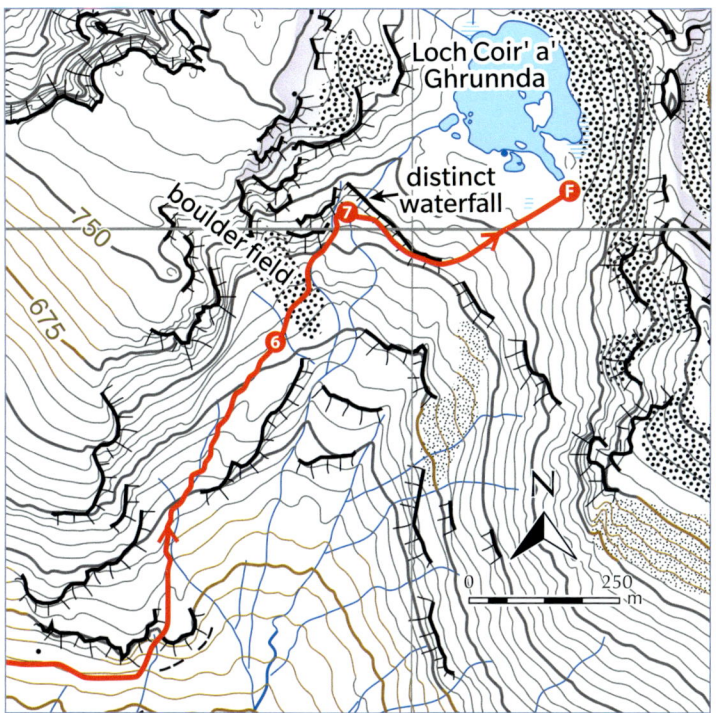

a boulder field of huge rocks then ascending left to the base of a parallel-sided gully, or continuing on the zigzag scree path above the boulder field then descending to the base of the gully.

The parallel-sided gully is left of steep slabs. Go up the gully then zigzag up scree and rocks parallel with the stream flowing down from the coire above.

7 Progress ahead is barred by steep cliffs and a distinctive waterfall. The easiest line is to head out right below the steep cliffs. Contour rightwards with a few short sections of scrambling. Continue heading right and upwards until **Loch Coir' a' Ghrunnda** is reached.

Alternatively, scramble up rocky steps to the left of the waterfall and continue up to **Loch Coir' a' Ghrunnda**.

From the loch, all three of the Southern Munros are within striking distance.

Sgurr nan Eag

Route	North Ridge
Grade	Grade 1
Peak height	924m

Sgurr nan Eag is the most southerly Munro on the Cuillin Ridge, and is little more than tough walking with some easy scrambling. The route has beautiful views down to Loch Coir' a' Ghrunnda and out to sea.

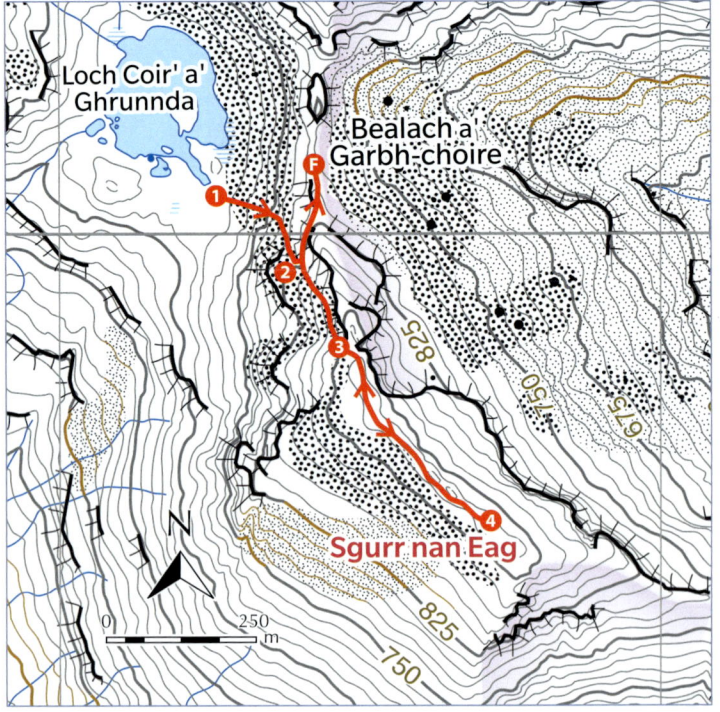

Sgurr nan Eag from Coir' a' Ghrunnda

Skye Munros Topo Booklet

❶ From the loch, head up the obvious scree slope. Initially the route crosses boulders but higher up a zigzag path works its way up the scree. The easiest line is to stay right (west) of the rocky ridge itself.

❷ Signs of a horizontal path head left. This will later be followed on the route to Bealach a' Garbh-choire and later Sgurr Dubh Mor. Head right and zigzag up scree and dirt.

❸ Easy scrambling leads up onto the more or less horizontal ridge. This leads to the summit which seems further away than the map suggests. There are a couple of false summits but you'll know you've reached the high point due to a large cairn on top of a small rocky outcrop.

❹ Scramble up to the huge cairn on the summit of **Sgurr nan Eag**.

Retrace your steps back along the ridge and descend the way you came.

Return to 2, and contour round along ledges to bypass the steep ridge and arrive at **Bealach a' Garbh-choire**.

View down to Coir' a' Ghrunnda and to Sgurr Alasdair from the ridge leading out to summit of Sgurr nan Eag

Route 4 – The Southern Three Munros

Sgurr Dubh Mor via Sgurr Dubh an Da Bheinn

Route	South ridge of Sgurr Dubh an Da Bheinn, then descend the east ridge of Sgurr Dubh an Da Bheinn. Ascend the south-west flank of Sgurr Dubh Mor
Grade	Grade 2 scrambling
Peak height	Sgurr Dubh an Da Bheinn 938m, Sgurr Dubh Mor 944m

Easy scrambling leads up Sgurr Dubh na Da Bheinn with short, rocky steps interspersed with walking.

❶ From Bealach a' Garbh-choire head north to the distinctive **Caisteal a' Garbh-choire** which juts up from the ridge. It and the surrounding boulders are made of an ultra-rough rock called peridotite.

Caisteal a' Garbh-choire is bypassed to the right (east).

The easiest and most straightforward way to reach Sgurr Dubh Mor is by traversing Sgurr Dubh an Da Bheinn. This involves a fair amount of height gain and loss so some people may prefer the alternative 'runners' route' described below.

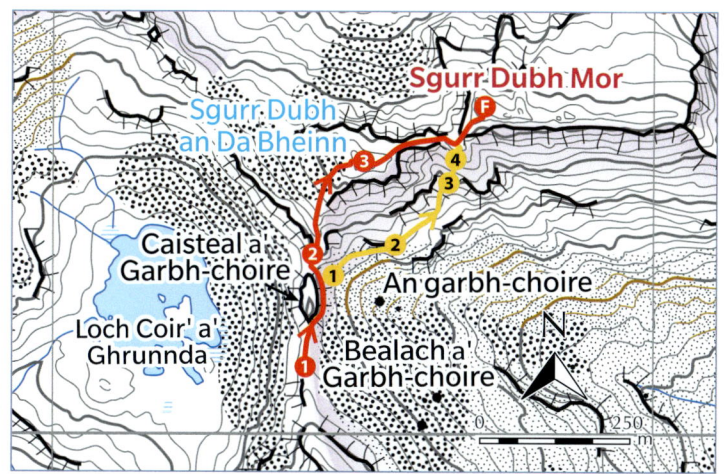

89

❷ **South ridge of Sgurr Dubh an Da Bheinn.** Grade 2 scrambling. Enjoyable scrambling on the rough peridotite. Work your way up enormous blocks and small cliffs, generally slightly to the Coir' a' Ghrunnda side. Head up just left of the ridge line until reaching a wide boulder-strewn ledge which is followed left. Continue working up, then head right to the summit of **Sgurr Dubh an Da Bheinn**.

The 'runners' route'

This alternative bypass heads directly out to Sgurr Dubh Mor from Caisteal a' Garbh-choire. It is much quicker and more direct and saves a fair amount of height loss/gain, but the terrain is complex with a lot of loose rock. If in any doubt as to your ability and/or the line of the route then it's best to head directly up Sgurr Dubh an Da Bheinn.

❶ Before the path around Caisteal a' Garbh-choire starts to ascend, turn right across boulders, descending then re-ascending. Initial boulder hopping leads to a bit of a path which passes above a fairly distinct yellow rock scar.

❷ From above the yellow scar, continue up a scree ramp. Descend and contour round to a slab/wall which seemingly prevents access to the gully above.

❸ The wall is a grade 2 scramble in a fairly exposed position. Ascend on the left side then cross horizontally rightwards to ascend a gully/chimney. At the top of the wall, descend slightly to the right and reach the base of a scree-filled gully.

❹ Carefully ascend the loose blocks and scree to break out rightwards and head up to the very obvious horizontal path to the right (south) of the col between Sgurr Dubh an Da Bheinn and Sgurr Dubh Mor. Walk along the path until you can see a fairly obvious brown slab which leads up to Sgurr Dubh Mor.

Main route

❸ Consider leaving your packs at Sgurr Dubh an Da Bheinn. From the summit, descend steeply but fairly easily to a stone bivi circle.

❹ Below this, options vary but the easiest is to stay left of the crest of the ridge by descending a gully. The base of this is blocked by rocks from a pillar which collapsed. Scramble down these, then climb up and right to traverse back onto the ridge proper.

❺ Descend easily to the col where a path leads horizontally out to the right. Follow this until an obvious brown slab is reached on the left.

❻ Scramble up the slab, then climb cracked rocks on the left to reach another path which curves around to the right in a horizontal fashion to reach a gully.

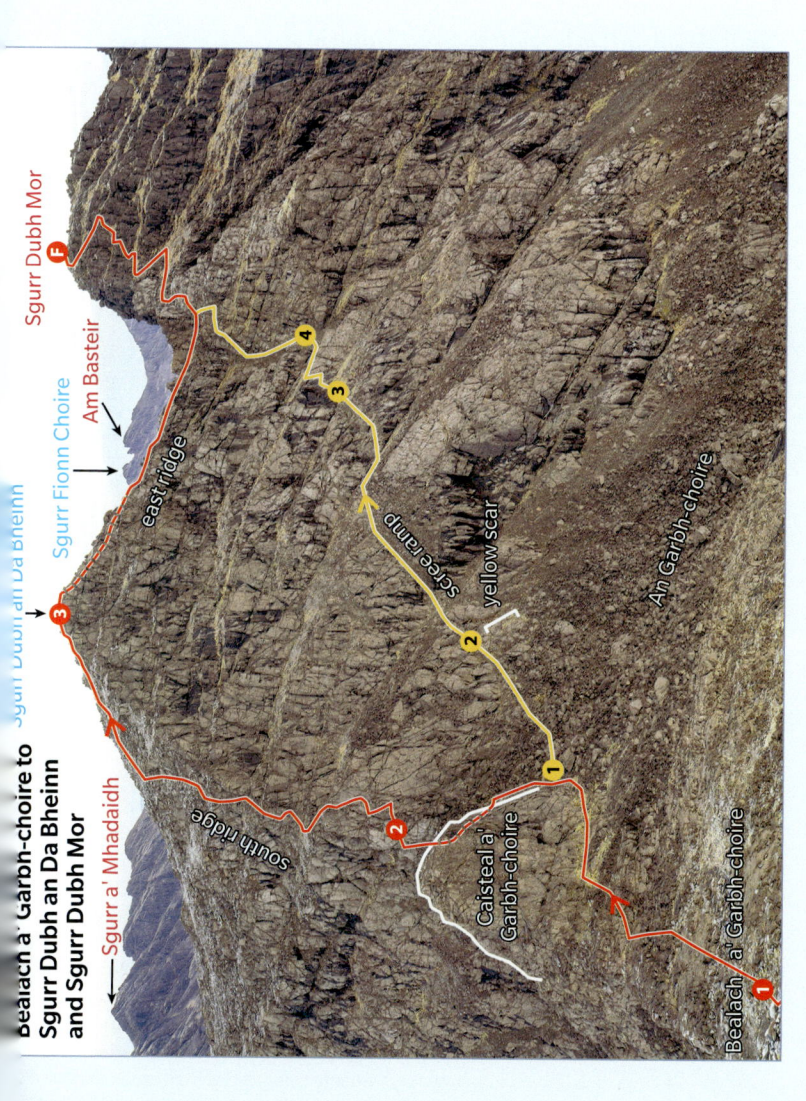

Sgurr Dubh an Da Bheinn to Sgurr Dubh Mor

An Garbh-choire

7 Ascend the gully via loose rock to a col.

8 From the col, a grass path heads rightwards beneath the summit block.
Follow the path right for a short way before cutting back left to ascend a series of corners and rocky steps to reach a slab.

9 The slab has very positive holds but is an awkward exit onto the ledges above (grade 2 scrambling). At the ledges, overhanging terrain to the left prevents access to easier terrain that leads to the summit. Above and right is an obvious triangular rock. Above this block is a horizontal rock ledge which bypasses the overhanging terrain and enables you to reach an area of grass.

Route 4 – The Southern Three Munros

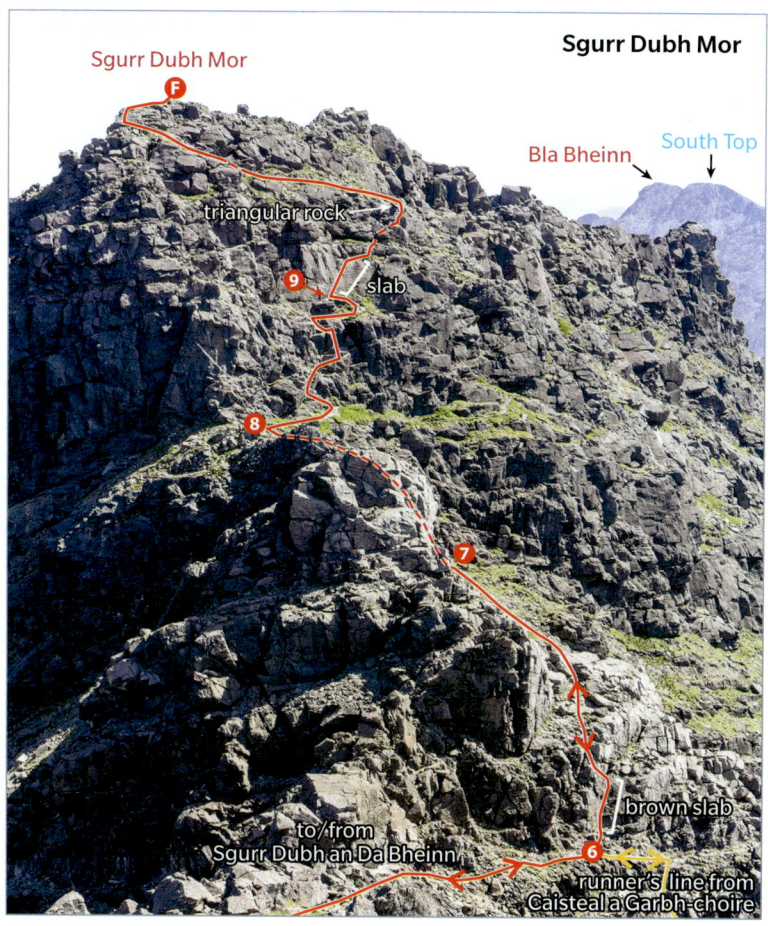

To reach easier terrain, ignore the ledge leading left and carry on ahead, climbing between rocks to reach a corner which leads back left to the easier terrain and a path. Follow the obvious line to just below the final summit block. Climb this to reach the summit cairn of **Sgurr Dubh Mor**.

Descent: Retrace the route to Sgurr Dubh an Da Bheinn.

Awkward slabs just before the summit of Sgurr Dubh Mor

Sgurr Dubh an Da Bheinn to Sgurr Alasdair

Route	Walking, then south-west flank of Sgurr Alasdair
Grade	Scrambling to grade 3
Peak height	993m

The first section involves easy scrambling and rough walking as you leave Sgurr Dubh an Da Bheinn. Easy scrambling leads to a scree path below the TD Gap which, in turn, leads to an awkward chimney on Sgurr Alasdair (grade 3 scramble) with exposed scrambling above.

Route 4 – The Southern Three Munros

❶ Leave the summit of Sgurr Dubh an Da Bheinn and descend the north-west ridge (grade 1), which is initially easy scrambling then becomes a walk to **Bealach Coir' an Lochain**.

❷ Take care in poor visibility since this area can be very disorientating. From the bealach, ascend a rocky ridge on the far side and continue along it for about 125m towards the TD Gap. Just before a small col, descend diagonally leftwards (on Coir' a' Ghrunnda side) to a short chimney that leads down to grass and scree. Contour round to the entrance to the **TD Gap**.

❸ Cross an obvious scree cone below the TD Gap. Follow the path above the scree slopes, contouring round to a bivi cave. (Sgurr Sgumain bivi cave can offer welcome shelter on a poor day. Above and right are distinctive pinnacles at Bealach Sgumain.) For those bagging Munro Tops, Sgurr Sgumain is within easy reach. For route description see Sgurr Sgumain.

❹ From the bivi cave head up towards the pinnacles at the bealach above, but after a few metres head out right and traverse to the base of a chimney. This is about 50m east and 20m lower than the bealach.

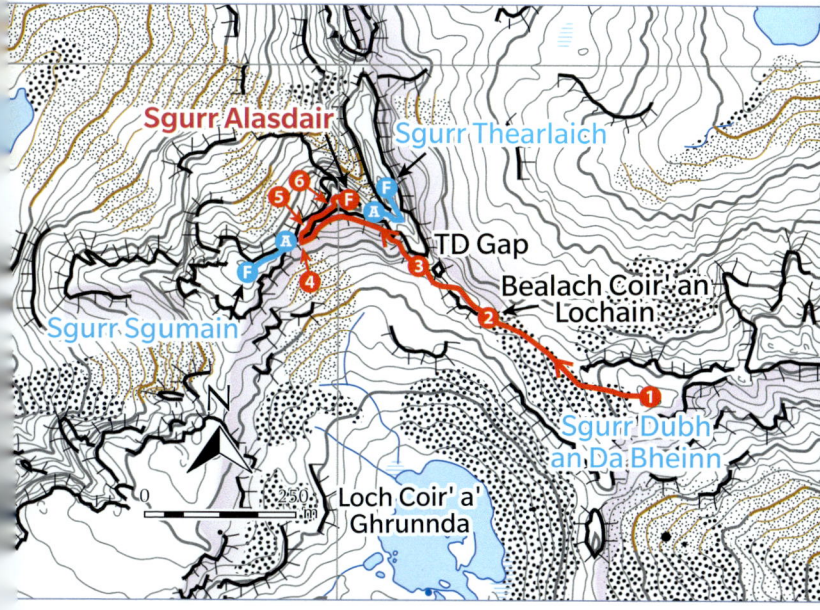

Sgurr Sgumain bivi cave

5 Scramble up to reach the chimney then climb it, exiting right at the top. The chimney looks worse than it actually is. Despite it being steep, the holds are very positive and with being enclosed, there is not too much sense of exposure. This is very much the crux of the route.

From the top of the chimney, the south-west flank is a bit devoid of features. Broken terrain interrupts short scrambling sections. Follow a line of weakness up to the right from the top of the chimney. Grooves and corners lead to an awkward step up a steep section of the corner. Continue heading up and right, taking the easiest line, then cut back left towards the south-west ridge.

6 A horizontal ledge leads back to the south-west ridge.

For those with a dislike of exposure, go along the ledge until just before the south-west ridge, then head directly up a series of steps and grooves to the summit.

For a more exposed and exhilarating finale, continue along the ledge and follow the south-west ridge to the summit of **Sgurr Alasdair**. This is very exposed since the ridge forms the division between Coir' a' Ghrunnda and Coire Lagan but the holds are large and positive.

Descent: See Sgurr Alasdair via the Great Stone Chute and south-east ridge for descent description. From the top of the Chute, the Munro Top of Sgurr Thearlaich is only a short distance away. For route description, see Sgurr Thearlaich.

South-west flank of Sgurr Alasdair

Sgurr Alasdair **F**

south-west ridge

south-east ridge & descent to Stone Chute

6

5

chimney

Route 4 – The Southern Three Munros

On the summit of Sgurr Alasdair after climbing the South West Flank.

Sgurr Sgumain

Route	North-east ridge
Grade	Grade 2 or 3
Peak height	947m

Sgurr Sgumain is a Munro Top situated off the main Cuillin Ridge. It is in an airy position high above both Coir' a' Ghrunnda and Coire Lagan and adjacent to the highest peak on Skye, Sgurr Alasdair..

See Sgurr Dubh an Da Bheinn to Sgurr Alasdair for map.

From Bealach Sgumain there are two routes to the summit:

🅐 Either ascend to the ridge between the pinnacles and the ridge leading up Sgurr Sgumain, then cross to the Coire Lagan side where a path contours round to a slab which must be crossed (grade 2 scramble). Then head upwards to a small col. Follow the north-east ridge to the summit of **Sgurr Sgumain**.

Or ascend to the ridge between the pinnacles and the ridge leading up Sgurr Sgumain. Initially follow the Coire Lagan side, then cross to the Coir' a' Ghrunnda side. Follow ledges which lead to some grade 3 scrambling to regain the ridge leading to the summit of **Sgurr Sgumain**.

A solitary figure on top of Sgurr Thearlaich with the top of the Great Stone Chute to the left and Sgurr Alasdair left again. Sgurr Mhic Choinnich far right.

Sgurr Thearlaich

Route	South ridge
Grade	Grade 3
Peak height	984m

The line of ascent is also the easiest descent route so keep this in mind as you climb.

See Sgurr Dubh an Da Bheinn to Sgurr Alasdair for map.

🅐 Steep cliffs bar access to Sgurr Thearlaich. The easiest route is to descend about 30m from the saddle down a zigzag path on the Coir' a' Ghrunnda side. Be careful not to descend too far because the scree drops off precipitously lower down.

Follow an easy traverse left along distinct strata to reach the actual crest of the south ridge. Above, the ridge narrows and the easiest line is on the right of the crest. Follow this to the summit of **Sgurr Thearlaich**.

Descent: Descend the same way then go down **The Great Stone Chute**.

Sgurr Thearlaich

Sgurr Thearlaich F

Sgurr Dubh Mor

Sgurr Dubh an Da Bheinn

route largely obscured and to the right of the crest

A

The Great Stone Chute

Sgurr Alasdair via the Great Stone Chute and south-east ridge

Start/finish	Car park at end of road immediately before Glen Brittle Campsite (NG 409 206)
Time	5–6hr
Distance	9.5km
Total ascent/descent	1050m
Grade	Grade 2
Peak height	993m
Warning	If you don't like scree then give this route a miss. With all the scree and loose rocks this is definitely a good place to be wearing a helmet, especially if there are other parties ahead of you.

This is a relatively straightforward ascent. It's not too technical, just hard work. The Great Stone Chute looks intimidating but will succumb to a determined effort. It's almost 400m of ascent, mostly up unstable scree where progress is measured by one step up followed by half a step down. The final section is grade 2 scrambling which may well come as a relief after the scree.

The route is very much of a 'go anywhere' nature. Many will be attracted to the obvious 'track' down the centre of the lower scree, but this is highly mobile and much better options are found by following the right-hand edge of the Chute.

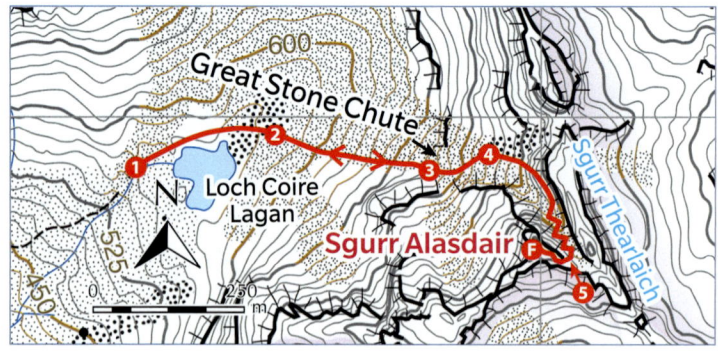

Higher up, the Great Stone Chute becomes more defined with steep rock walls

Follow the path from Glen Brittle Campsite up to Coire Lagan (see The Approach to Coire Lagan).

❶ Go around the edge of **Loch Coire Lagan**. Cross a stream flowing into the loch, then go past stone-walled shelters to reach the base of the **Great Stone Chute**.

❷ Take the right edge of the scree, hugging the rocks at the edge of the Chute.

The centre of the scree is the obvious line and many will opt for it, but it's much harder work than the route up the edge. (Most people will take the centre line on descent.)

❸ Move away from the right wall and head back left to ascend the left side of the Chute.

❹ Continue up the left side. Higher up, a zigzag path leads to the rocky col in between Sgurr Alasdair and Sgurr Thearlaich.

❺ From the stone shelter at the col, head right and follow a path round and then up the east ridge (grade 2). Head up and right over short steps to reach the slabby ridge overlooking the Great Stone Chute. These slabs can be slippery in the wet so be aware of the huge drop to the right.

A bit of airy ridge scrambling then leads to the summit of **Sgurr Alasdair**.

Descent: Retrace your route to the col and descend the Chute, then return to Glen Brittle.

Route 5
Bla Bheinn and the South Top

Start/finish	NG 561 216. Park at the John Muir Trust car park on the west shore of Loch Slapin. Leave Broadford on the B8063, drive to Torrin then continue for 3.5 km to the car park.
Time	4–5hr
Distance	8.5km
Total ascent/descent	919m
Grade	Rough walking with only minimal scrambling
Peak height	928m
Warning	Navigation on the upper part can be tricky in poor visibility. Potentially difficult/impossible to cross the river if it is in spate.

This is one of the easiest Cuillin Munros, with a good path for much of the way and minimal scrambling. There is lots of scree and rocks, and at times the route is ill-defined so can be a challenge in poor visibility. Bla Bheinn offers stunning views in every direction and is a good vantage point to spot the Munros on the main Cuillin Ridge.

Looking ahead to Bla Bheinn with Clach Glas to the right

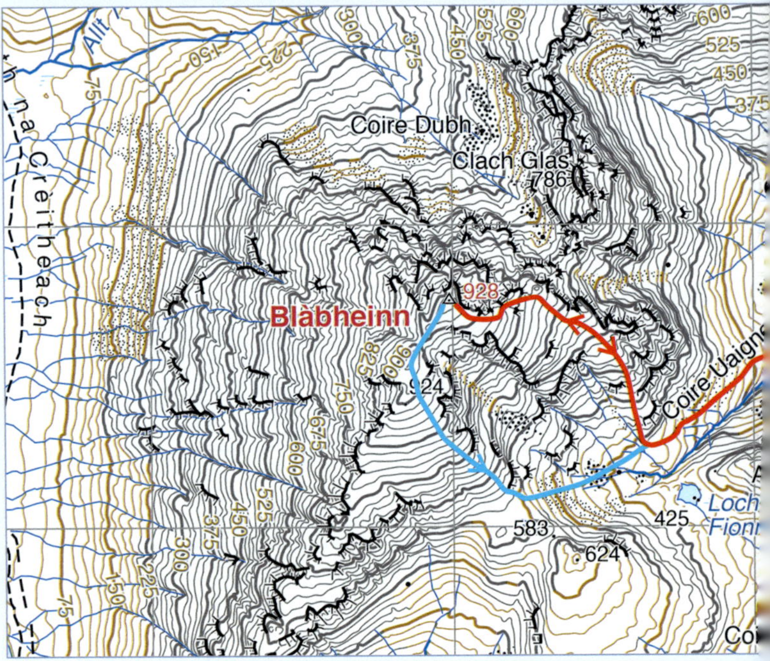

Skye Munros Topo Booklet

View down to Loch Fionna Choire with Loch Slapin far left

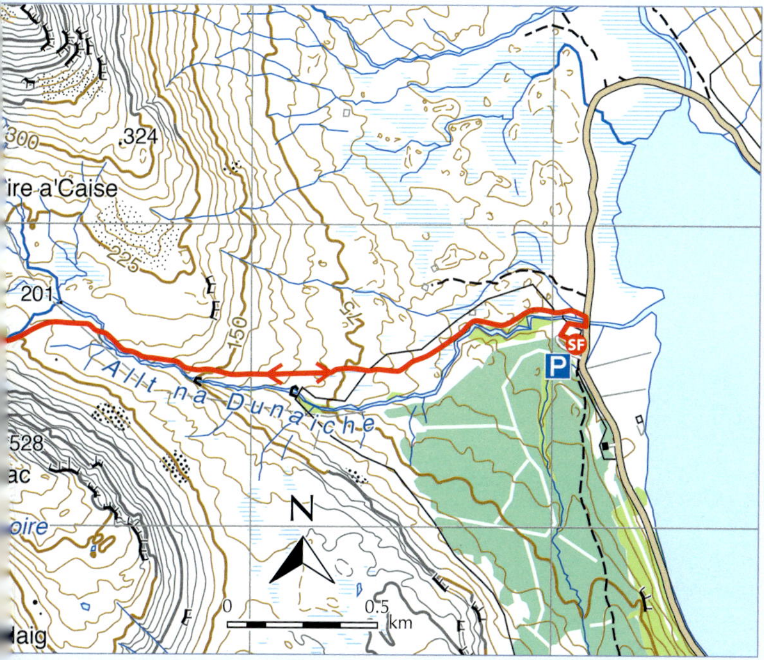

Route 5 – Bla Bheinn and the South Top

High up on Bla Bheinn with a view to the neighbouring Clach Glas

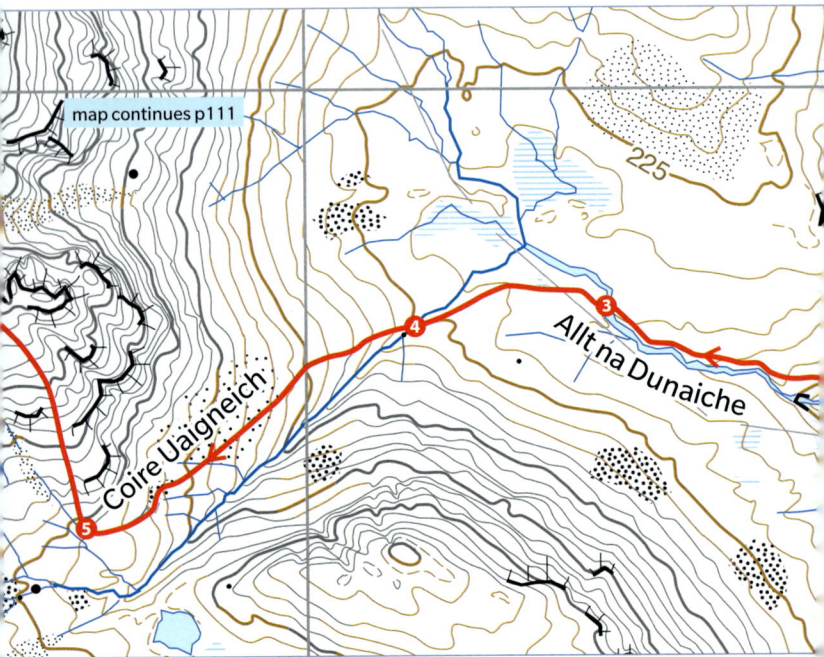

Bla Bheinn and the South Top

1 Leave the car park and cross the **Allt na Dunaiche** by the road bridge you have just driven over.

2 Turn sharp left along a good path which follows the stream up towards Bla Bheinn and Clach Glas. The path leads past waterfalls with views ahead to Bla Bheinn.

3 Cross the Allt na Dunaiche to reach the far bank. This can be problematic if water levels are high.

4 The path heads up into **Coire Uaigneich** following a stream. Higher up, the rocky path gives way to grass and the terrain levels off.

5 The route now turns right to head up the east ridge. If you come to a huge boulder then you have gone about 150m too far.

The ascent of the east ridge is technically straightforward, but in poor visibility finding the right line can be challenging. When looking up to the

Route 5 – Bla Bheinn and the South Top

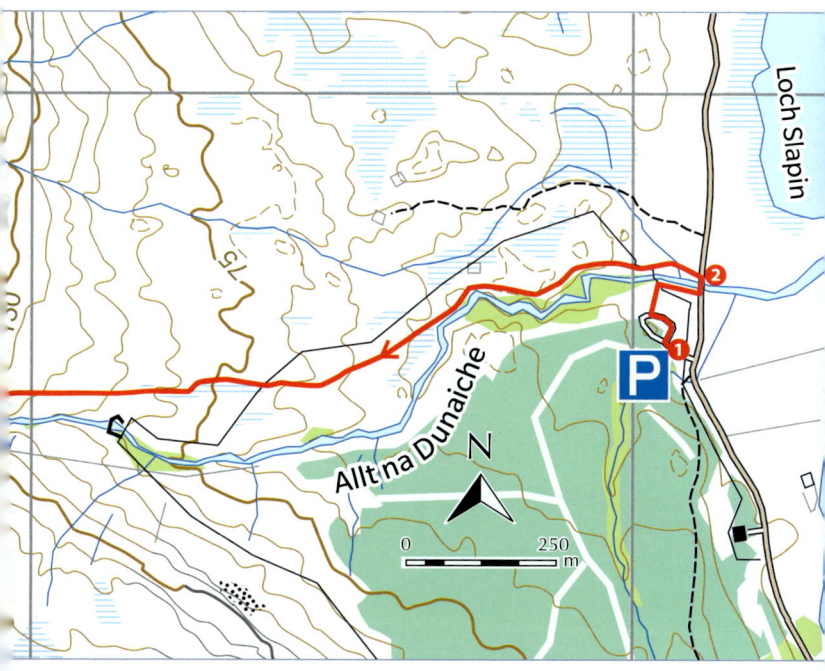

east face, there is a large gully of scree to your left. This leads up to the gully dividing the main and south summits. To the right of the scree gully is a steep rocky buttress, then there are two parallel slot-like gullies. Next on the right, rock/grass buttresses head up to the east ridge which forms the skyline.

Left and lower than the base of the slot-like gullies, a cairn indicates a badly eroded path that heads up a grass spur. Follow the path left to avoid crags.

Continue up and right to cross a scree slope and grass. This leads to a short, steep scree gully which cuts up between the crags.

6 This gully is very loose and can be avoided by easy scrambling to the left.

From the top of the gully, another eroded path on grassy slopes gives way to yet more rock and scree. At about 600m, the path comes close to the edge of the coire with cliffs to the east. Bear slightly right to enjoy views across the coire.

Route 5 – Bla Bheinn and the South Top

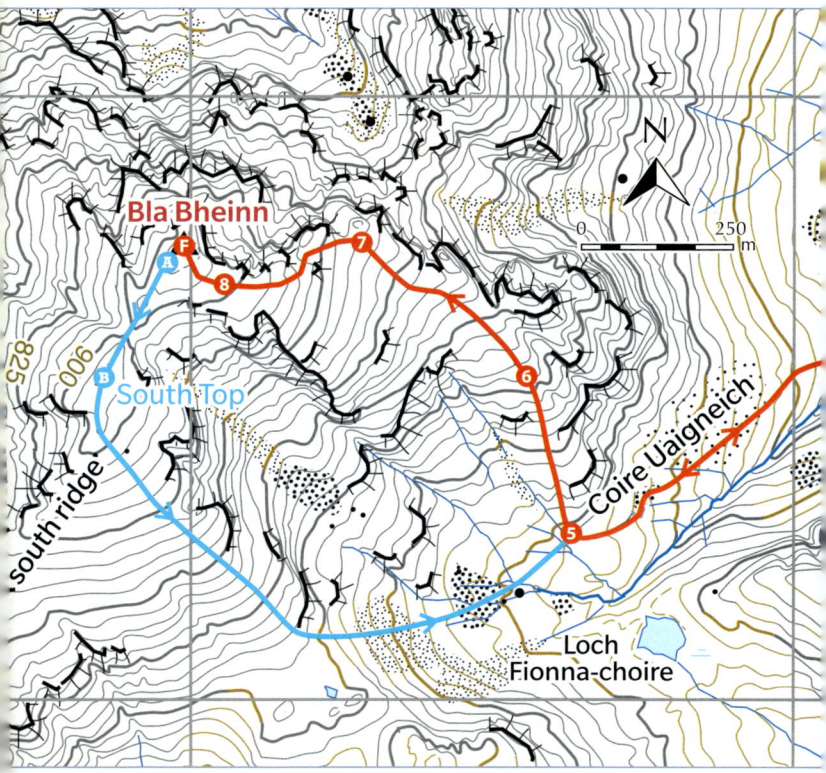

7 Follow the more defined ridge, first in a north-westerly then a westerly direction.

8 The terrain becomes increasingly rocky. The obvious line channels you towards a narrow gully which involves a bit of easy scrambling up rocks at its top.

Easier terrain follows. The path zigzags up rocks and scree to reach the summit of **Bla Bheinn**. This is one of only two trig points in the Cuillin, the other being on Bruach na Frithe.

Descent: The easiest way is to return via the ascent route.

The South Top (924m, grade 2)

While on the main summit it is worth considering bagging the South Top which is only a short distance away.

Bla Bheinn with Clach Glas centre and the Corbett, Garbh-bheinn on the left

Allow about 30min total to go out to the South Top and back to the trig point.

🅐 From the trig point, descend south-west to the col above the top of **Great Gully**. Ahead, a rocky prow protects the South Summit. The prow can either be taken by ledges to the left on the Loch Slapin side or directly. Both are grade 2 scrambles.

🅑 Reach the **South Top**, 924m.

Descent: The most obvious route is to return to the trig point and descend the east ridge.

The broad south-east ridge can be used as an alternative. A cairned path heads down from the South Top through rocks and scree. Start off in a southerly direction below a crag on the crest of the south ridge. Next, switch to descending south-easterly via scree paths and short rock steps to reach a wide grass col by a wee lochain. Head east down a path into **Coire Uaigneich** and meet the path you originally ascended to gain the east ridge.

NOTES

NOTES

Download the GPX files

All the routes in this guide are available for download from:

www.cicerone.co.uk/1204/GPX

as standard format GPX files. You should be able to load them into most online GPX systems and mobile devices, whether GPS or smartphone. You may need to convert the file into your preferred format using a conversion programme such as gpsvisualizer.com or one of the many other such websites and programmes.

When you follow this link, you will be asked for your email address and where you purchased the guidebook, and have the option to subscribe to the Cicerone e-newsletter.

www.cicerone.co.uk

LISTING OF CICERONE GUIDES

BRITISH ISLES CHALLENGES, COLLECTIONS AND ACTIVITIES

Great Walks on the England Coast Path
Map and Compass
The Big Rounds
The Book of the Bivvy
The Book of the Bothy
The Mountains of England and Wales
   Vol 1 — Wales
   Vol 2 — England
The National Trails
Walking the End to End Trail
Cycling Land's End to John o' Groats

LAKE DISTRICT

Bikepacking in the Lake District
Cycling in the Lake District
Joss Naylor's Lakes, Meres and Waters of the Lake District
Lake District Winter Climbs
Lake District: High Level and Fell Walks
Lake District: Low Level and Lake Walks
Mountain Biking in the Lake District
Outdoor Adventures with Children — Lake District
Scrambles in the Lake District — North
Scrambles in the Lake District — South
Trail and Fell Running in the Lake District
Walking The Cumbria Way
Walking the Lake District Fells
   — Borrowdale
   — Buttermere
   — Coniston
   — Keswick
   — Langdale
   — Mardale and the Far East
   — Patterdale
   — Wasdale
Walking the Tour of the Lake District

NORTH-WEST ENGLAND AND THE ISLE OF MAN

Walking the King Charles III England Coast Path: North West
Walking the King Charles III England Coast Path: North West
   — Cumbria Map Booklet
   — Lancashire and Merseyside Map Booklet
Cycling the Pennine Bridleway
Walking the Pennine Way
Walking the Pennine Way Map Booklet
Isle of Man Coastal Path
The Lune Valley and Howgills
Walking in Cumbria's Eden Valley
Walking in Lancashire
Walking in the Forest of Bowland and Pendle
Walking on the Isle of Man
Walking on the West Pennine Moors
Walking the Ribble Way
Hadrian's Wall Path
Hadrian's Wall Path Map Booklet

The Coast to Coast Cycle Route
The Coast to Coast Map Booklet
The Coast to Coast Walk

NORTH-EAST ENGLAND, YORKSHIRE DALES AND PENNINES

Walking the Dales Way
The Dales Way Map Booklet
Cycling the Reivers Route
Cycling the Way of the Roses
Cycling in the Yorkshire Dales
Great Mountain Days in the Pennines
Mountain Biking in the Yorkshire Dales
The Cleveland Way and the Yorkshire Wolds Way
The Cleveland Way Map Booklet
The North York Moors
Trail and Fell Running in the Yorkshire Dales
Walking in County Durham
Walking in Northumberland
Walking in Northumberland
Walking in the North Pennines
Walking in the Yorkshire Dales
   — North and East
   — South and West
Walking St Cuthbert's Way
Walking St Oswald's Way and Northumberland Coast Path

DERBYSHIRE, PEAK DISTRICT AND MIDLANDS

Cycling in the Peak District
Dark Peak Walks
Scrambles in the Dark Peak
Walking in Derbyshire
Walking in the Peak District
   — White Peak East
   — White Peak West

SOUTHERN ENGLAND

20 Classic Sportive Rides in South East England
20 Classic Sportive Rides in South West England
Bikepacking — South East Gravel
Cycling in the Cotswolds
Mountain Biking on the North Downs
South West Coast Path Map Booklet
   — Vol 1: Minehead to St Ives
   — Vol 2: St Ives to Plymouth
   — Vol 3: Plymouth to Poole
Suffolk Coast and Heath Walks
The Cotswold Way
The Cotswold Way Map Booklet
The Kennet and Avon Canal
The Lea Valley Walk
The Lea Valley Walk
The North Downs Way
North Downs Way Map Booklet
The Peddars Way and Norfolk Coast Path
The Pilgrims' Way
The Ridgeway National Trail

The Ridgeway Map Booklet
The South Downs Way
The South Downs Way Map Booklet
The Thames Path
The Thames Path Map Booklet
The Two Moors Way
Two Moors Way Map Booklet
Walking Hampshire's Test Way
Walking in Essex
Walking in Kent
Walking in London
Walking in Norfolk
Walking in the Chilterns
Walking in the Cotswolds
Walking in the Isles of Scilly
Walking in the New Forest
Walking on the North Wessex Downs
Walking on Dartmoor
Walking on Guernsey
Walking on Jersey
Walking on the Isle of Wight
Walking the Dartmoor Way
Walking the Jurassic Coast
Walking the Sarsen Way
Walking the South West Coast Path
Walks in the South Downs National Park

WALES AND WELSH BORDERS

Cycle Touring in Wales
Cycling Lon Las Cymru
Great Mountain Days in Snowdonia
Hillwalking in Shropshire
Mountain Walking in Snowdonia
Offa's Dyke Path
Offa's Dyke Map Booklet
Scrambles in Snowdonia
Snowdonia 30 Low-level and Easy Walks
   — North
   — South
The Cambrian Way
The Pembrokeshire Coast Path
Pembrokeshire Coast Path Map Booklet
The Snowdonia Way
The Wye Valley Walk
Walking Glyndwr's Way
Walking in Carmarthenshire
Walking in Gower
Walking in Pembrokeshire
Walking in the Brecon Beacons
Walking on Gower
Walking the Severn Way
Walking the Shropshire Way
Walking the Wales Coast Path

SHORT WALKS SERIES

15 Short Walks in Dumfries and Galloway
15 Short Walks in Perthshire North — Pitlochry, Aberfeldy and Dunkeld
15 Short Walks in the Scottish Borders
15 Short Walks in the Trossachs — Callander and Aberfoyle
15 Short Walks on the Isle of Mull
15 Short Walks on the Isle of Skye

15 Short Walks on the Orkney Islands
15 Short Walks on the Shetland Islands
15 Short Walks Hadrian's Wall
15 Short Walks in the Lake District
— Keswick, Borrowdale and Buttermere
— Windermere Ambleside and Grasmere
— Coniston and Langdale
15 Short Walks in Arnside and Silverdale
15 Short Walks in the Ribble Valley
15 Short Walks in Nidderdale
15 Short Walks in Northumberland — Wooler, Rothbury, Alnwick and the coast
15 Short Walks in the Yorkshire Dales
— Grassington, Skipton, Malham and Ilkley
— Sedbergh, Kirkby Lonsdale and Ingleton
15 Short Walks in the Peak District — Bakewell and the White Peak
15 Short Walks in the Peak District — Edale and the Hope Valley
15 Short Walks on the Malvern Hills
15 Short Walks Cheddar and the Mendips
15 Short Walks in Cornwall
— Newquay and the North Coast
— Falmouth and the Lizard
— Land's End and Penzance
15 Short Walks in Norfolk — Broads and Coast
15 Short Walks in South Devon — Salcombe, Brixham and the coast
15 Short Walks in the South Downs — Brighton, Eastbourne and Arundel
15 Short Walks in the Surrey Hills
15 Short Walks on Dartmoor North — Okehampton and Chagford
15 Short Walks on Dartmoor South — Ivybridge and Princetown
15 Short Walks on Exmoor
15 Short Walks on the Isle of Wight
15 Short Walks Winchester
15 Short Walks in Bannau Brycheiniog — Brecon Beacons
15 Short Walks in Pembrokeshire — Tenby and the south
15 Short Walks in the Forest of Dean

SCOTLAND

Ben Nevis and Glen Coe
Cycling in the Hebrides
Cycling in the Hebrides
Cycling the North Coast 500
Great Mountain Days in Scotland
Mountain Biking in Southern and Central Scotland
Mountain Biking in West and North West Scotland
Not the West Highland Way: A Mountain High Way
Scotland
Scotland's Best Small Mountains
Scottish Wild Country Backpacking
Skye Munros
Skye's Cuillin Ridge Traverse
The Borders Abbeys Way
The Hebridean Way
The Hebrides
The Isle of Skye
The Skye Trail
The Southern Upland Way
The West Highland Way
West Highland Way Map Booklet
Walking Ben Lawers, Rannoch and Atholl
Walking in the Cairngorms
Walking in the Pentland Hills
Walking in the Scottish Borders
Walking in the Southern Uplands
Walking in Torridon, Fisherfield, Fannichs and An Teallach
Walking Loch Lomond and the Trossachs
Walking on Arran
Walking on Harris and Lewis
Walking on Jura, Islay and Colonsay
Walking on Mull, Coll and Tiree
Walking on Rum and the Small Isles
Walking on the Orkney and Shetland Isles
Walking on Uist and Barra
Walking Rum and the Small Isles
Walking the Cape Wrath Trail
Walking the Corbetts
 Vol 1 — South of the Great Glen
 Vol 2 — North of the Great Glen
Walking the Fife Pilgrim Way
Walking the Galloway Hills
Walking the Great Glen Way
Walking the Great Glen Way Map Booklet
Walking the John o' Groats Trail
Walking the Munros
 Vol 1 — Southern, Central and Western Highlands
 Vol 2 — Northern Highlands and the Cairngorms
Winter Climbs in the Cairngorms
Winter Climbs: Ben Nevis and Glen Coe

ALPS CROSS-BORDER ROUTES

100 Hut Walks in the Alps
Alpine Ski Mountaineering Vol 1 — Western Alps
Hiking the Tour of Monte Rosa
The Karnischer Hohenweg
The Tour of the Bernina
Trail Running — Chamonix and the Mont Blanc region
Trekking Chamonix to Zermatt
Trekking in the Alps
Trekking in the Silvretta and Ratikon Alps
Trekking Munich to Venice
Trekking the Tour du Mont Blanc
Tour du Mont Blanc Map Booklet
Walking in the Alps

FRANCE, BELGIUM AND LUXEMBOURG

Camino de Santiago — Via Podiensis
Chamonix Mountain Adventures
Cycling London to Paris
Cycling the Canal de la Garonne
Cycling the Canal du Midi
Mont Blanc Walks
Mountain Adventures in the Maurienne
Short Treks on Corsica
The GR5 Trail — Through the French Alps
The GR5 Trail — Vosges and Jura
The Moselle Cycle Route
Trekking in the Vanoise
Trekking the Cathar Way
Trekking the GR10
Trekking the GR20 Corsica
Trekking the Robert Louis Stevenson Trail
Via Ferratas of the French Alps
Walking in Provence — East
Walking in Provence — West
Walking in the Auvergne
Walking in the Briançonnais
Walking in the Dordogne
Walking in the Haute Savoie: North
Walking in the Haute Savoie: South
Walking on Corsica
Walking the Brittany Coast Path
The GR5 Trail — Benelux and Lorraine
Walking in the Ardennes
The River Loire Cycle Route
The River Rhone Cycle Route
Cycling the Route des Grandes Alpes

PYRENEES AND FRANCE/SPAIN CROSS-BORDER ROUTES

Shorter Treks in the Pyrenees
The Pyrenean Haute Route
The Pyrenees
Trekking the Cami dels Bons Homes
Trekking the GR11 Trail
Walks and Climbs in the Pyrenees

SPAIN AND PORTUGAL

Camino de Santiago: Camino Frances
Coastal Walks in Andalucia
Costa Blanca Mountain Adventures
Cycling the Camino de Santiago
Mountain Walking in Mallorca
Mountain Walking in Southern Catalunya
Spain's Sendero Historico: The GR1
The Andalucian Coast to Coast Walk
The Camino del Norte and Camino Primitivo
The Camino Ingles and Ruta do Mar
The Mountains Around Nerja
The Mountains of Ronda and Grazalema
The Sierras of Extremadura
Trekking in Mallorca
Trekking in the Canary Islands
Trekking the GR7 in Andalucia
Walking and Trekking in the Sierra Nevada
Walking in Andalucia
Walking in Catalunya — Barcelona
Walking in Catalunya — Girona Pyrenees
Walking in the Picos de Europa
Walking La Via de la Plata and Camino Sanabres
Walking on Gran Canaria
Walking on La Gomera and El Hierro
Walking on La Palma
Walking on Lanzarote and Fuerteventura

Walking on Tenerife
Walking on the Costa Blanca
Walking the Camino dos Faros
Portugal's Rota Vicentina
The Camino Portugues
Walking in Portugal
Walking in the Algarve
Walking in the Algarve
Walking on Madeira
Walking on the Azores
Cycling the Ruta Via de la Plata

SWITZERLAND

Switzerland's Jura Crest Trail
The Swiss Alps
Tour of the Jungfrau Region
Trekking the Swiss Via Alpina
Walking in Arolla and Zinal
Walking in the Bernese Oberland — Jungfrau region
Walking in the Engadine — Switzerland
Walking in Ticino
Walking in Zermatt and Saas-Fee

GERMANY

Hiking and Cycling in the Black Forest
The Danube Cycleway Vol 1
The Rhine Cycle Route
The Westweg
Walking in the Bavarian Alps
The Elbe Cycle Route

POLAND, SLOVAKIA, ROMANIA, HUNGARY AND BULGARIA

The Danube Cycleway Vol 2
The High Tatras
The Mountains of Romania

SCANDINAVIA, ICELAND AND GREENLAND

Hiking in Norway
  — North
  — South
Trekking the Kungsleden
Trekking in Greenland — The Arctic Circle Trail
Walking and Trekking in Iceland

SLOVENIA, CROATIA, SERBIA, MONTENEGRO AND ALBANIA

Hiking Slovenia's Juliana Trail
Mountain Biking in Slovenia
The Islands of Croatia
The Julian Alps of Slovenia
The Mountains of Montenegro
The Peaks of the Balkans Trail
The Slovene Mountain Trail
Walking in Slovenia: The Karavanke
Walking the Julian Alps of Slovenia
Walks and Treks in Croatia

ITALY

Alta Via 1 — Trekking in the Dolomites
Alta Via 2 — Trekking in the Dolomites
Day Walks in the Dolomites
Italy's Grande Traversata delle Alpi
Ski Touring and Snowshoeing in the Dolomites
The Way of St Francis: Via di Francesco
Trekking Gran Paradiso: Alta Via 2
Trekking in the Apennines
Trekking the Giants' Trail: Alta Via 1 through the Italian Pennine Alps
Via Ferratas of the Italian Dolomites
  — Vol 1
  — Vol 2
Walking Gran Paradiso National Park
Walking in Abruzzo
Walking in Italy's Cinque Terre
Walking in Italy's Stelvio National Park
Walking in Sicily
Walking in the Aosta Valley
Walking in the Dolomites
Walking in Tuscany
Walking in Umbria
Walking Lake Como and Maggiore
Walking Lake Garda and Iseo
Walking on the Amalfi Coast
Walking the Cammino Materano
Walking the Via Francigena Pilgrim Route
  — Part 1
  — Part 2
  — Part 3
  — Part 4
Walks and Treks in the Maritime Alps

IRELAND

The Wild Atlantic Way and Western Ireland
Walking the Kerry Way
Walking the Wicklow Way

INTERNATIONAL CHALLENGES, COLLECTIONS AND ACTIVITIES

Europe's High Points
Pocket First Aid and Wilderness Medicine

AUSTRIA

Innsbruck Mountain Adventures
Trekking Austria's Adlerweg
Trekking in Austria's Hohe Tauern
Trekking in Austria's Stubai Alps
Trekking in Austria's Zillertal Alps
Walking in Austria
Walking in the Salzkammergut: the Austrian Lake District

MEDITERRANEAN

Trekking in Greece
Walking and Trekking in Zagori
Walking and Trekking on Corfu
Walking on the Greek Islands — the Cyclades
Walking in Cyprus
Walking on Malta

HIMALAYA

8000 metres
Annapurna
Everest: A Trekker's Guide
Trekking in the Indian Himalayas
Trekking in the Karakoram

NORTH AMERICA

Hiking and Cycling the California Missions Trail
Hiking the Pacific Crest Trail
The John Muir Trail

SOUTH AMERICA

Aconcagua and the Southern Andes
Hiking and Biking Peru's Inca Trails
Trekking in Torres del Paine

AFRICA

Climbing Toubkal
Kilimanjaro
Walking in the Drakensberg
Walks and Scrambles in the Moroccan Anti-Atlas

NEW ZEALAND AND AUSTRALIA

Hiking the Overland Track

CHINA, JAPAN AND ASIA

Hiking and Trekking in the Japan Alps and Mount Fuji
Hiking in Hong Kong
Japan's Kumano Kodo Pilgrimage
Trekking in Bhutan
Trekking in Ladakh
Trekking in Tajikistan
Trekking in the Himalaya

TECHNIQUES

Fastpacking
The Mountain Hut Book

MINI GUIDES

Alpine Flowers
Navigation

MOUNTAIN LITERATURE

A Walk in the Clouds
Abode of the Gods
Fifty Years of Adventure
The Pennine Way — the Path, the People, the Journey
Unjustifiable Risk?

For full information on all our guides, books and eBooks,
visit our website:
www.cicerone.co.uk

CICERONE

Trust Cicerone to guide your next adventure, wherever it may be around the world...

Discover guides for hiking, mountain walking, backpacking, trekking, trail running, cycling and mountain biking, ski touring, climbing and scrambling in Britain, Europe and worldwide.

Connect with Cicerone online and find inspiration.

- buy books and ebooks
- articles, advice and trip reports
- GPX files and updates
- regular newsletter

cicerone.co.uk